Islam and Civil Society

Edited by

Hedieh Mirahmadi

Published by

WORDE

World Organization for Resource Development & Education

WORDE

ISBN: 1-930409-30-3

Library of Congress Cataloging-in-Publication Data

Mirahmadi, Hedieh
   Islam & Civil Society: collection of essays on Islam and democracy from the International Conference of Islamic Scholars December 2004/ edited by Hedieh Mirahmadi
  p. cm.
   ISBN 1-930409-30-3
  1. Islam & Civil Society.   2. International Conference of Islamic Scholars.   I. Title.
  BP190.5.S3K3 2005 297.4--dc22   2005003109

Cover Artwork and Graphic Design by Christina Matsoukis

Published and Distributed by:
WORDE (World Organization for Resource Development and Education)
4200 Wisconson Ave. NW
#106-339
Washington, DC   20016
Tel: (202) 595-1355 Fax: (202) 318-2582
Email: staff@worde.org
Web: http://www.worde.org

Islam and Civil Society

Edited by
Hedieh Mirahmadi

Table of Contents

Editor's Notes

*T*his book is specifically designed for laypersons and other non-Muslim readers. As such, we have often replaced Arabic terminology with English translations, except in instances where Arabic terms are crucial to the tone and substance of the text. In such instances, we have included transliterations or footnoted explanations.

For those who are familiar with Arabic and Islamic teachings, we apologize for the vastly simplified transliterations. Our experience is that unfamiliar symbols and diacritical marks make for diffcult reading by laypersons; as such, please indulge this compromise between accuracy and accessibility.

Holy Traditions of Prophet Muhammad appear without full chains of transmission, but are firmly established and should be familiar to and immediately accepted on sight by the vast majority of Muslim readers, and certainly by religious scholars.

Where gender-specific pronouns such as "he" and "him" are applied in a general sense, it has been solely for the flow of text, and no offense is intended to women readers.

Preface

by Hedieh Mirahmadi

The first International Conference of Islamic Scholars (ICIS) was held in Indonesia in February 2004. The conference was hosted by Nahdatul Ulama (NU) and the Indonesian Ministry of Foreign Affairs. There was an impressive list of Muslim scholars from around the world who participated, addressing many of the critical issues affecting Muslims today. The essays presented here are part of the follow up seminar of the International Conference of Islamic Scholars held in Jakarta from December 21 to December 24 of 2004.

The World Organization for Resource Development and Education (WORDE) used its combined religious, academic and political expertise to increase the sustainability and effectiveness of the work already begun by the ICIS project. We gathered some of the most progressive and world-renowned Islamic scholars, politicians and academics that have a demonstrable ability to analyze the historical background of a particular aspect of civil society in an Islamic context and provide cogent policy recommendations for change.

In addition to **WORDE**, the conference was supported by several prominent institutions. Each of the organizations listed below made a critical contribution to the conference's success.

STATE ISLAMIC UNIVERSITY JAKARTA (UIN): The UIN is a fully accredited university teaching both Islamic sciences and secular disciplines. Its Director, Professor Dr. Azyumardi Azra, is internationally recognized for his leadership in the area of Islam and democracy. The university hosted a seminar which included presentations from the Minister of Education of Malaysia and the Crown Prince of Perak, Malaysia.

NAHDATUL ULAMA (NU): Founded in Indonesia, NU is one of the largest Muslim NGOs in the world and boasts of approximately 40 million members. They are in charge of thousands of *pesantrans* (religious schools) across the country and are willing partners for change. The chairman of NU, Shaykh Hasyim Muzadi, was also chosen as the first chairman for the ICIS Secretariat. As the ideologue of the party, he is the hope of NU political aspirants. Theologically a Muslim moderate with both English and Arabic language skills, he supports the peaceful coexistence of Islam and democratic ideals.

THE ISLAMIC SUPREME COUNCIL OF AMERICA (ISCA): A religious organization in the US dedicated to promoting Sufi Islam in modern society, ISCA provided a substantial part of the funding and administrative support for the event.

YAYASAN HAQQANI FOUNDATION, INDONESIA: The Haqqani Foundation is a local Indonesia NGO that provided logistical support for the conference.

My special thanks go to Shaykh Muhammad Hisham Kabbani for the boundless energy, wisdom and inspiration he gave to this project. I would also like to thank His Excellency Dato Hishamuddin Tun Hussein, Minister of Education of Malaysia, and His Royal Highness Prince Raja Muda Nazrin Shah ibni Sultan Azlan Shah who took time from their personal schedules to address the conference.

Finally, my sincere appreciation goes to the WORDE and ISCA staff—including our graphic designer Christina Matsoukis, without whom this book would not be possible—and the wonderful participants of the conference who provided the vision and hope for the future.

Introduction

by Hedieh Mirahmadi

*T*he struggle for ideological primacy within Islam is a fight that only Muslims themselves can wage, but the moderates are struggling for access to the public square. Muslim societies the world over have been intimidated, oppressed and manipulated by extremist ideologues and financiers for almost a half century. The only surviving civic culture you see today is the corrupt networks of government leaders and/or the Islamist infrastructure. In our quest for "liberty for all", we must level that playing field for the mainstream Muslims who have no means to effectively contribute in the "marketplace of ideas".

Across the Middle East and the Muslim world writ large, there has been a systematic attempt to divorce local populations from their cultural heritage and drive them into a militant Islamic movement that survives on fear and hatred of the "other." Militant Islamist ideologues have spent billions of dollars to radicalize young Muslim men, and their societies as a whole, by convincing them that the West is engaged in a war against Islam. These extremists foster a belief system that relies on destroying everything outside of it. In this regard, it is no different than fascism and communism, and if not similarly confronted, will undermine any other democratic initiatives.

Extremists are best able to overpower a community when no opposite civic institutions exist. Effective civil society institutions instill the traditions and culture of a society and serve as a vanguard against imported hostile ideologies. Take for example the American experience with communism. Though the Soviets spent a fortune on promoting communist ideology in the US, the greatest defense against it was indigenous civic institutions like free media, think tanks, religious establishments, and social organizations. In the Middle East, dictatorship has prevented the growth of independent civic institutions that reflect the character and culture of the people. The only institutions that exist are ones that are manipulated by the government and/or funded by extremists because they solidify the control of the central government. The prospects for maintaining or establishing democratic systems in such a climate are bleak. Effective, independent civil society infrastructure creates the civic culture necessary to support real democratic values of freedom of expression, religion, and association.

For example, prior to the importation of strict extremist interpretations of Islam, it was common in throughout the Middle East and Asia to patronage the arts of cultural folk dances and songs. It was a way of forging unity between Muslim and non-Muslim citizens in a social and friendly atmosphere. Unfortunately, neither the state nor private citizens realized the consequence of discontinuing these traditions when the radicals insisted they stop. Reinvigorating these local practices is one way of countering the controlling influence of the extremists and bolstering the legitimacy of Muslim clerics and community leaders who allow them. This affects the struggle between moderation and radicalism by providing the public space for citizens who are desperate for alternatives to the violent indoctrination of the extremists. Muslims and non-Muslims alike can come together in a way that forges societal cohesion based on mutual affinity of a shared culture and acceptance of religious diversity.

The greatest assistance the US can provide to this evolution into self determination for the Middle East is funding civil society initiatives that reinvigorate cultural traditions that are not at war with the West and do not subjugate women. We need to help generate the public space where tolerant and open-minded Muslim clerics can reintroduce things like poetry, art and music to their communities. We need to establish meeting places for rising democratic activists to discuss their theories with fellow citizens and to develop civil society institutions that are legitimate by local and international standards.

Recent events in Lebanon, known as the "Cedar Revolution", prove the universal desire of freedom lives in all people. We need to nurture that aspiration in a way that leads to a permanent culture of independence. We need to combine indigenous democratic ethics, with modern notions of free society, to transform communities at the grassroots. As a result of the increased familiarity with the ideals of a democratic society– expressed in a way that is compatible to those of the West though not identical to them – we can decrease the anti-Americanism and anti-Westernism that is so prevalent in the Muslim world today.

In the Islamic world, opinion makers have a critical role to play in this global battle between extremism and moderation. The traditions of the Islamic faith provide religious leaders unique access to the microphone and the ability to influence the masses. Primary opinion makers in Islamic societies are:

- Religious scholars – critical to establishing moderation and whose religious verdicts (*fatwas*) which often direct national policy

- Academics – affect direction of political and social change through research and debate

- Government functionaries – the vanguard for policy implementation

- Imams – primary local dispensers of major policy changes

- Business leaders – influence the grassroots

- Media personalities – able to spread religious verdicts widely

Unfortunately, until now, access has been given almost exclusively to the most extreme of these voices because of the exorbitant private funding they enjoy and the encouragement of local governments. Amidst the loud chorus of extremist voices, those of moderation are often drowned out. Yet democratic citizens of the United States and Europe are keenly aware of the need to help change this dynamic and provide access to more tolerant voices, who advocate change and modernity. As America seeks to encourage democracy and civil society institutions in

Afghanistan, Iraq and the larger Islamic world, it is reaching out to these forces of moderation.

It is in this backdrop that we held the follow-on seminar of the International Conference of Islamic Scholars in Jakarta, Indonesia December 2004. The conference provided leading Muslim voices of change their chance to assert the following:

- Islam is a universal faith with a history of tolerance, equality, and multiculturalism.

- Modern day applications of Islamic doctrine are *not* incompatible with democracy and the development of vibrant, effective civil society institutions.

- Recent political upheavals and historical mistakes allowed extremism to displace tolerant Islam and it is up to the people to reject that trend and reverse it.

- Moderate political, religious and community leaders must collectively and individually provide their societies with progressive, modern interpretations of Islam in order to overcome religious extremism, as well as the overwhelming poverty and oppression that plagues most Muslim societies today.

The format of the papers generated by the conference were designed to not only provide the requisite interpretations of the most critical issues of Islam and democracy, but to also provide policy recommendations that will assist NGO's, governments and international bodies alike in implementing civil society infrastructure and educational reform in Muslim majority societies.

The papers presented by Dr. Hashim Kamali and Shaykh Muhammad Hisham Kabbani are traditional "fatwa style" religious rulings. Both scholars cited laws of the Quran, traditions of the Prophet, and combined that with historical context and legal extrapolation, to prove the case for democratic values and civilian government in Islam. The science of classical Islamic jurisprudence is very similar to the American legal system in that the jurist relies on "black letter" law and case precedence to argue why his legal premise is valid. Shaykh Kabbani and Dr. Kamali follow that methodology to clarify important issues like the rules of military engagement and civil dimensions of governance in Islam. The arguments presented demonstrate that not only are Islam and democracy compatible, but that individual freedoms and the rule of law are cornerstones of real Islamic values.

Dr. Kamali's paper includes brief descriptions of the various forms of government in the Islamic world throughout history. The varying perspectives and models demonstrate that no one system is more credible than another and that modern societal evolution can justify new systems. Remember, neither the Quran nor the traditions of the Prophet specified the exact nature and character of government. In fact, a minority of jurists have even argued for no government at all based on the reason that the Sharia is silent on the matter.

It is important to note as well that the modern idea of a 'Sharia State" was introduced by Ibn Tamiyya in the 14th century, over 700 years after the death of the Prophet Mohammed. After the fall of the caliphate in Baghdad, he proposed this new interpretation of what an Islamic government should be. Ibn Tamiyya's created this system based on his own juridical analysis of Islamic text and has no greater claim to authenticity than the other systems, especially since there was no historical precedence for the model he suggested. In fact, much of Ibn Tamiyya's analysis was so contrary to prevailing norms that he was often referred to as a heretic. His revolutionary doctrine was later revived by the puritanical ideologue, Mohammed Ibn Wahhab, who used it as grounds to abolish the legal traditions of the past and to impose his one narrow minded interpretation of Islamic government we see throughout the Muslim world today. Ibn Taymiyya and Mohammed Ibn Wahhab are the two most recognized theologians of the Salafi movement.

On the subject of reviving the caliphate, which many Islamists argue for today including the most extreme factions like Al Qaeda, the majority of Sunni jurists assert that a khilafa [a single ruler] for the Islamic world can no longer exist because there is no territorial unity of Muslims lands. Therefore, scholars reasoned that secular monarchs were valid forms of government since the underlieing principles of Islam would be maintained i.e. rationality and group consensus, as well as maintaining people's welfare. Though the monarch was viewed as the "protector" of faith, he was not a religious figure himself and he appointed a "religious council" to address matters of religion. Today, in the example of the modern nation state, the rationale for secular leadership still applies. The government is responsible for the civilian matters of property rights, courts, military and foreign policy, while religious tribunals could effectuate the personal and social affairs of their respective communities.

Muslims living in existing or burgeoning democracies, grappling with issues of politics and government, can draw from many legal traditions of the past that bolster the case for civilian government and the universal standards of freedom. However, the most important Islamic legal tradition of all is the one that allows society to evolve, interpret, and adapt the laws of the public to suit life's changing circumstances. We cannot be intimidated by the rhetoric of extremists who claim there is only one right answer. Knowledge is power and courage is priceless.

Conclusion

Today is a crucial turning point for Islam and Muslims: in its relations with the non-Muslim world; with one another, and in its responsibility as one of the world's great religions. If as a culture and civilization, united purely by faith, Muslims fail to come forward with an approach that puts responsibility for its destiny squarely on its own shoulders, they cannot expect a bright future.

For too long, as a religious community, Muslims have sought the path of blame and failed to undertake the hard work of self-critique, analysis and adjustment. It is for such purposes this conference was convened. As the follow-on to the International Conference of Islamic Scholars that took place in February 2004, this gathering of distinguished scholars and politicians deliberated issues of the gravest concern to the Muslim community and to the world at large.

In doing so, they sought an opening by which to initiate the process of critical self-examination, and yes, self- purification, without which the Muslim world will undoubtedly fall further into self-doubt, disintegration and alarm before the bewildering array of social, political, and spiritual changes taking place in the world today.

Address at Jakarta Islamic University

December 22, 2004

by
His Excellency
Dato Seri Hishamuddin Tun Hussein

Minister of Education, Malaysia

Address at Jakarta Islamic University
December 22, 2004

by His Excellency Dato Seri Hishamuddin Tun Hussein

*L*adies and Gentlemen:

I am greatly to be honored to have been invited to address you here today. The theme of this conference could not be more relevant. The programmatic idea behind this conference is something the world, and not just the Muslim world, needs: in an environment ruled by polarized and extreme views, it is high time that we heard from moderate and peaceful Muslims voices. The moderate voice of Islam, which would represent the vast majority of Muslims, is too often drowned out by more strident ones. It is time that moderate, peaceful and progressive Islam spoke up.

The participants of this conference are united in their conviction that it is time to articulate an alternative which has always been available, an alternative which represents the mainstream of Islamic history. In articulating this alternative, this moderate, progressive and peaceful Islam, an Islam for all ages and places. You now want to get from tracing its architecture to laying its bricks, from retelling its glorious past to doing something to make it a present possibility.

You seek good examples of policy and practice. What, as Muslims should we do to start building prosperous, moderate and progressive Muslim countries?

The world in which we, as Muslims, have to live and flourish does not suddenly narrow down to some particular set of purely Muslim issues as soon as we come together as Muslims. Muslim countries do not exist in a different world from non-Muslim ones. Despite what some people might be tempted to imagine, they never did.

I am not a scholar, and I can only draw from the experience of Malaysia. Malaysia is a young country, and our experience is limited. Each Muslim society must find its own answers. Nevertheless we can try to learn from each other. With humility, then, let me share with you how we answer this question for Malaysia.

I will sketch the larger context in which we act as Muslims. It is in this broader context that we in Malaysia are conscious of ourselves as Muslims. It is in this broader context that we propose and conduct policy.

Muslims in Malaysia are a small majority of just over 60% in a country that has about a tenth the population of Indonesia.

Our smallness, and hence our vulnerability, may help account for why Muslims in Malaysia have constantly to be oriented toward others and sensitive to their context. Domestically we live and work side by side with a very visible and vibrant non-Muslim communities. Internationally, we are a small country with an open, export oriented economy. We are the largest exporter of semiconductors in the world. We are the fourteenth largest trading nation. We have to keep our finger on the pulse of the rest of the world. We must understand how to work with others both at home and abroad. We must be able to play our part in chains of collaborative production that stretch across the globe, among people of different languages, backgrounds and faiths. We must adapt quickly to changes in our environment. We must be willing to absorb and deploy scientific and technological knowledge. Our survival depends on it.

Browse any history book and you will see that the peoples of these lands have always relied on trade. Our ancestors were merchants and seafarers. We can look back to the sultanate of Melaka, which was the nexus of seaborne trade between India and China in the 14th century. Melaka was a thriving, cosmopolitan, multi-cultural polity in its heyday, with travelers and settlers from Persia, Arabia, the Indian Subcontinent, China and the islands of present day Indonesia. As far back as you trace our way of being Muslim, Malay or Malaysian, we have lived and worked and traded with peoples of many lands, entire communities of whom, as you can see, have also made Malaysia their home. Our time and place has always been shared with others.

Islam in Malaysia, if I may speak so broadly, is pragmatic, open, and by its very nature progressive. Others may look down on us for our mixed heritage. They may regard our having grown up in the rough and tumble of sharing and exchange with diverse peoples near and far as a mark against us. We are not pure enough for some. We are not pure enough in our religious expression for those who like their world in monochrome. But I maintain that we have reason to stand proud, not just as Malaysians but also as Muslims. We have managed - through hard work at the unglamorous, exhausting, often thankless, task of nation-building - to create a society where men and women of different religions and races can live in harmony together, work together, bring up their families and plan for their future with confidence. I can speak for my fellow Malaysians. I feel, when I say that this is not merely a compromise forced upon us by the special circumstances of our nationhood.

By now, you will note, our orientation towards racial and religious harmony is not just how we *had* to be, it is how we would *choose* to be. By now too, we have the confidence to recognize that what we have done in this country is also a Muslim achievement. We as Muslims in Malaysia are proud of our record of having fostered a peaceful and progressive multi-religious society in a modern world in which such examples are all too rare. We have chosen the rough and tumble of making a society work in Southeast Asia in the twenty first century rather than try to conform ourselves to a mythical model of purity. We educate, persuade and cajole people to seek their common prosperity rather than their mutual destruction.

All this work for a unity among ourselves that is also open to the world draws on, a practice of Islam which is at peace with itself and with the world; a practice of Islam which takes the time and place in which the Muslim finds herself, the neighbors she finds around her, her non-

Muslim friends, not as obstacles, or accidents, or incidentals of history, but as the gift of the Divine. Out of such materials we are called to fashion a peaceful society which gives glory to Allah swt.

This is an approach that we are now trying to make normative- We hope to teach it to our children. In the words of our Prime Minister YAB Dato' Seri Abdullah Ahmad Badawi this approach "values substance and not form." It seeks to make Muslims understand that such things as the improvement of our institutions, and the pursuit of balanced and comprehensive economic development is important work, and it is *jihad*. Because we value substance rather than form we take our starting point in the concrete and often messy circumstances in which we as Muslims find ourselves rather than in some ideal context of the imagination.

In Malaysia, a country of many races and many religions, unity is the first task. Without unity, nothing else would be possible for us as a society. As a Muslim I see the promotion of unity as a task enjoined by the principle of the unity of god and of creation, or *tauhid*: under one God, a united humanity, a united creation.

As Minister of Education, I am answerable not just to Muslims but to teachers, parents, and children who also happen to be Christians, Buddhists, Hindus, Sikhs and practitioners of local religions.

What I have outlined, then, is a context: for acting as a Muslim in a Muslim majority country. In that pragmatic context, issues such governance and the fight against corruption, rural development, the improvement of health care are approached and tackled with the best means available and in collaboration with many partners. Most of our problems cannot be solved without collaboration with our non-Muslim friends.

Ladies and Gentlemen:

In the light of this approach, if you asked me to outline some Muslim issues that we are concerned with in the Ministry of Education, they would be:

a) The relative underdevelopment of our rural Schools, and the lower attainments of children from those schools

b) The provision and management of the best Information Technology services and infrastructure we can afford to all our schools.

c) Bridging a looming digital divide which must not be allowed to take root as knowledge divide

d) Making our National schools the cradle of a diverse, yet united people, at peace with themselves and with one another.

e) Training our young people to be discerning users of media; helping them build internal firewalls based on our religious values against the unworthy or degrading content that will be streaming in their direction through the internet and the mass media.

The substance, if not the form, of every one of these issues is also religious, for Islam demands a radical commitment to knowledge and to the pursuit of knowledge.

Islam is a religion based upon knowledge. In the end it is the knowledge of the Oneness of God combined with faith and total commitment to Him that redeems us. The text of the Qu'ran invites us to use our intellect, to ponder, to investigate and to know, for the goal of human life is to discover the Truth which is none other than worshipping God in His Oneness. The Hadith literature is also full of references to the importance of knowledge. We are taught sayings of the

Prophet s.a.w. such as "Seek knowledge from the cradle to the grave", and "Verily the men of knowledge are the inheritors of the prophets".

To be a Muslim is to be a creature in the one world created by the One God. This is an immensely practical; situated view of the world. I am, and could only be, a Muslim from a particular time and place with its own history. In Malaysia, the Muslim finds himself in the role of peacemaker and a creator of value in a diverse, cosmopolitan, open society in which there are multiple links and ties between cultures.

We are summoned to a universal *ummah*, but we are summoned as we are, with all our ties and responsibilities to those with whom we live day by day; in other words, with all that binds us to those beside us in this world, with the links forged by the One Creator. We do not think that our non-Muslim neighbors are only accidentally or temporarily beside us. We do not wish them away; however challenging it may be to live side by side.

Unless I am deeply mistaken, this acceptance of our situated ness, this openness to our neighbor; our world, and the practical demands of that world, is fundamental to Islam. The great Islamic societies fashioned their faithfulness out of local material; the social and cultural features of the place and time in which they found themselves. The great Islamic societies were hosts to diverse peoples, traded with all and sundry, drew from diverse influences, and maintained their unity without eradicating their diversity. The ones that did not regressed.

Ladies and Gentlemen:

The path to the transformation of Muslim majority societies, then, is not exotic or magical. I do not think there is a unitary Muslim formula to fit all the wonderful diversity of Muslim societies out there. What we need instead are good Muslims committed to the hard work, the creative thinking, the *jihad*, of building peaceful and prosperous societies. It requires a willingness to engage with the rest of the world because this is what it takes to succeed in a globalized world economy.

It requires investment in our people. In Malaysia we are trying to reform and re-tool our education system to foster a more creative, adaptive and technologically literate citizenry. We must put the very highest priority on Education, and we must be careful that we raise our children to be effective in this world.

We need to foster in our children the higher order skills of analyzing, synthesizing and managing information. We know we need people who can prosper under unpredictable and quickly changing conditions. We know we need people who can communicate and work well with others. It is an Education which will prepare Muslims who can truly be God's *kalifah* in this world.

Having begun by nothing that the Malaysian experience is limited, let me now say why it may nevertheless be useful to others. The reason is that globalization is making the Malaysian context I described more familiar to other countries.

National populations everywhere are becoming more culturally-religiously and ethnically diverse: The UNDP's latest Development Report describes a kind of time bomb of ethnic diversity. It points out that from indigenous people in Latin America to ethnic groups in Africa and immigrants in Western Europe, many people are now mobilizing along ethnic, religious, racial and cultural lines- This is a process hastened along by the spread of democracy, advances in communication and the increasing pace of international migration. The report warns that unless we are able to build inclusive, culturally diverse societies we will be torn apart by the destructive effects of identity politics. We should set ourselves the challenge of building inclusive, culturally diverse societies that are also Muslim societies.

Societies are becoming increasingly inter-connected with each other via global economic, cultural and social movements. As telecommunications and air travel shrinks distances between countries, even large societies like Indonesia will not be able to shield themselves from global movements in people, ideas and capital. We had a chance to learn this lesson together the hard way in 1997.

However, if we look at our own heritage in Malaysia, in Indonesia and in much of the rest of Southeast Asia, we find that we have always lived with greater ethnic diversity and in greater interconnectedness with one another than people in other parts of the world. This also happens to have been the context for the rise of Islam in Southeast Asia.

But many of the places in which Islam has flourished were, like Malaysia and Indonesia, multi-ethnic and multi-religious trading communities situated at the borders or contact points between civilizations. Islam has had some of its most glorious moments not in homogenous environments but seemingly far-flung, multi-cultural environments such as Central Asia, Granada, Moghul India and the Ottoman Empire.

Insya Allah, a reinvigorated Islam, sure of itself, open to the world, and rich in knowledge, will also rebuild such splendor one day in our own "far flung comer" of the world.

The Ummah:
Challenges of the New Realities

by
His Royal Highness
Prince Raja Muda Nazrin Shah
ibni Sultan Azlan Shah

Crown Prince of Perak, Malaysia

The Ummah:
Challenges of the New Realities

by HRH Prince Raja Muda Nazrin Shah ibni Sultan Azlan Shah

Ladies and Gentlemen:

It is a very special privilege to be here today and I thank the organizers for the invitation to this platform, to join such eminent scholars and thinkers, representing some of the finest minds of our generation. I am able to take comfort in the fact that this is not just any Conference of Scholars but a Conference of Islamic Scholars. I take it therefore I am addressing my Muslim brothers in the spirit of brotherhood enjoined on us by our common religion. Seminars have become the all too common currency of today's intellectual discourse: We are in danger of Conference fatigue. But a very unique bond differentiates our deliberations today, united as we are in Islam.

2. Appropriately assembled in the world's largest Muslim country; we are a microcosm of the global Ummah to which we all owe our allegiance. It is a very timely opportunity because we desperately need to confront the Muslim Dilemma besetting us in this 21st Century. The Ummah is a giant conglomerate of countries with rich and diverse histories. The glue that binds them is Islam. But the prevailing impression of them today is that most are backward, mired in poverty and deprivation, weak, enfeebled and lacking in any form of cohesion or leadership.

3. Unfortunately it is Muslims in particular whom the world equates with the violent terrorism that holds the world to ransom and keeps us in perpetual fear. For this, however unfairly and indiscriminately, Islam itself is stigmatized.

4. This paper attempts to address the core challenge of restoring Muslim legitimacy- to give back pride and confidence to our peoples. To revitalize and renew the Ummah, it will take a social and economic

transformation that will leapfrog centuries of developmental inertia. We will need our moral compass to guide us through the complex jungle that is the 3rd Millennium. If renewal is accepted as imperative it will be premised on an economic resurgence; but one able to combine both the global dynamics of the present age with the unchanging tenets of Islam, its eternal verities and the principles of Islamic justice. Even though political and social systems have changed to suit the contemporary world, nevertheless our Muslim identity and our Muslims spirit remain intact. These were forged long ago in the Golden Age of the 9th to the 13th Centuries when Islam led the world in science and learning. Today this remains our inspirational model. Whilst we may aim, for now, to revive and rejuvenate the present generation of Muslim countries, ultimately we may again aspire to restore the glory of Islam.

5.   The precedent is there. Islam changed the nomadic feuding Arab tribes of the pre-Islamic period into a united, highly organized, sophisticated people. They built a great civilization based on learning and knowledge that extended from Spain to China. They added new fields of scholarship like astronomy and algebra. Muslim physicians and scientists contributed much to the advancement of medicine. They developed the use of metals and the skills and tools of navigation. Great libraries were set up in Cordoba and, yes, in Baghdad. This prompts some pretty rueful thinking today. Islam was the catalyst that energized the Middle Eastern people to their unchallenged eminence in that bygone age. Here then is the classic case study for today's Muslims to study and emulate. They showed us the way. We need to draw inspiration from this heritage to chart the future destiny of the Ummah.

6.   Sadly however, the Islamic world after its centuries of distinction has gone into a long and steep decline. After the collapse of the Turkish Ottoman, Muslims became divided and weakened. Only the splendid architecture survived monuments to our former glory. To know how far behind we have come, we need to analyze our history.

7. Why did we lose out? I come now to my main thesis - that we missed out on the Renaissance, the period of Enlightenment and above all we

missed out on the Industrial Revolution. We lost thereby a crucial stage in the evolution of human civilization and one that is ongoing to this day where a nation's prosperity and stage of development are linked to its level of industrialization.

The Industrial Revolution completely passed most of us by with disastrous consequences. It was Britain that started the new phenomenon but it was the fledgling America which was to exploit it to the full. We were pre-empted by the New World.

8. Man's progress can be charted in clear phases. We were very much part of the first - the Agricultural Age. We irrigated our farms, built our roads, developed the appropriate science and technology needed for the infrastructure that would farther develop an agrarian society. Let's take our own part of the world. Asia is not only the world's newest but the oldest region. South East Asia was a recognizable entity, even then, when the virtue of agriculture was first discovered through rice cultivation.

9. This part of the world was blessed, and still is, by a wealth of strategic natural resources, prized and coveted products like rubber, tin, minerals, oil, sugar and rice. These made us prey to domination and subjugation by outside powers. Ironically whilst our commodities were in great demand, we ourselves failed to capitalize on them fully which would have meant making the vital transition to the Industrial Revolution. Asia served only as the backyard of the newly industrialized countries of the West- a supplier of raw materials, relegated to be hewers of wood and carriers of water for the colonial masters.

10. Despite the vast resource endowments they possess, many Muslim countries are still underachievers, falling even further behind in an increasingly competitive and sophisticated world. How did all this happen? One school of thought suggests they lost their lead in civilization as a narrow religious conservatism gained ground, preoccupied with the next life not this one. Muslim societies became inward looking. Some religious scholars questioned the study of non-religious subjects

requiring Muslims to be learned in religion only, as the sole qualification to earn merit in the afterlife, the "akhirat". In the most extreme cases, having condemned and discarded the: study of science, mathematics, engineering and other "worldly" subjects they rejected the products of this worldly knowledge. Electricity, the printing press, automobiles were regarded as "haram" and initially forbidden. By the time Muslims came to understand the importance of modern industry they had been left far behind. From now on the pressing concern was one of catch up.

11.   The 20th Century introduced a different handicap. It spelt a particular disaster for the Islamic world caught in a cycle of political unrest and civil strife often instigated by outside powers. Muslims have no recourse but to take charge of their own destinies, not through politicizing religion but by economic renewal and human development to bring us level with the present civilization. While the Ummah advocates meaningful spiritual and intellectual advancement and strives to bring about political stability, our contention is that at the same time the importance of economic development cannot be ignored. This is the theme of the present paper. . Economics and education will also be needed to drive the engines of growth we seek. Education especially is required to change the present mindset. Modernity, innovation and technology have to be absorbed in all their relentless advance. A receptive mentality on the part of Muslims is a prerequisite of managing change. The pace and scale of change are today more rapid, profound and far reaching than ever before in history.

12.   The task in hand will have to be played out against a backdrop of the new realities of an increasingly borderless and globalizing world.

13.   What follows is an examination of the specific Muslim situation in the context of this globalizing international economy, the challenges and the problems, and the prognosis for a way forward and for the desired catch up.

14.   First the statistics. There are more than 1.2 billion Muslims on the planet dispersed world wide. The Islamic community of nations

reflected in then membership of OIG represents 57 countries heterogeneous in terms of political systems, economic structures, and ethnicity. The economic performance of many OIG countries has been poor. Based on the World Development Report 2005 about 46% of ole members can be classified as low income economies. Amongst low income economies world wide, about 43% are ole members. In 2001, ole countries constituted some 20% of the world's population but generated only 5% of the world's nominal GDP. Many still rely on agriculture or primary commodities as their source of wealth with low levels of industrialization and technological diffusion. Poverty is rampant. Per capita income is often abysmal. The picture is bleak. This may be obscured to a degree by a few high profile Muslim economies, the oil producers especially, but these are a handful. For many Muslim countries, the hidden social deficit is a low life expectancy, high infant mortality, low adult literacy.

15. Looking for a means to bring the backward amongst us into the 21st century globalization may well provide us our opportunity, whilst the abundant natural resources with which we have been blessed provide the means. Making the most productive use of these mandates globalizing our economies to achieve their true potential. At the individual country level some would find it very difficult to even attempt this. If we were to take the more remote areas it would be asking a traditional, simple, timeless village society -to break into a world of sophisticated technology. This would be almost tantamount to expecting them to accomplish overnight a miniature version of the Industrial Revolution they missed before.

16. However - individually we may be weak, but collectively we can be strong. The answer lies in coordinated effort, to build together a global Islamic presence that is a fully-paid up member of the world economy. This calls for a renewed impetus towards greater integration of our economic strategy - greater trade among Muslim countries, a pooling of skills and technology.

17. Because of the likely psychological barriers there will be a need to convince the more conservative that religion and economic progress

are not mutually exclusive and there is nothing to stop us pursuing achievement in this life, in worldly terms. The Prophet (PBUH) showed the way - the route of trade and business. He was himself a merchant. The Quran advocates peace and plenty as part of Allah's bounty to be shared by all. There is nothing in the Islamic code of life that says we must put off the fruits of our labors until the afterlife. To the contrary they are to be enjoyed here on earth. Economic wellbeing and the moral code go hand in hand. No one should be deprived of the basic necessities of life as promised by Allah. The present imbalance in society between the haves and the have-nots whereby the rich and powerful exploit the poor and the weak runs counter to Islamic belief. Wealth should be better distributed - circulated to all parts of society as blood circulates to all parts of the body like Malaysian policy of growth with distributive justice is a case in point. Our New Economic Policy, the NEP, a socio economic Program was implemented in the context of an expanding economy so that no one in society would experience any sense of economic deprivation.

18. The theological compatibility of religion and commerce is an accepted proposition worldwide. We hear that a lot, for instance, of the Protestant work ethic. Other races such as the Jews, the Quakers, the Parsees and the Jains have become noted for their business acumen. In Malaysia too, we had our own brand of the work ethic, only we looked East and emulated the Japanese. The latter taught us something else. Their commercial and management success was unique in being achieved without sacrifice of their cultural identity. To this we can also aspire, retaining our Islamic values whatever the context and demands of business.

19. Among the Abrahamaic religions, Islam is the least hostile to commerce. After all Muslim countries produced many 'of the great seafarers and the traders of the past and thus today ours are very open, hospitable economies. The Straits that separate our two countries, Indonesia and Malaysia, was historically a great sea-lane for the spice trade and remains one of the busiest thoroughfares in the modern world, the route for much of the oil traffic and the gateway between

East and West. It was traders who first brought Islam to our shores, through peaceful commerce not conquest.

20. The problem with development and the desire for catch up is that rising aspirations may then outstrip performance. But there are Muslim countries of respectable standing in the modern economic order, which furnish a demonstration effect.

21. Today Malaysia and Indonesia, as role models of development, demonstrate above all else that economic development, modernization and technology are not incompatible with Islam. They prove the value of opening up the contemporary economy to the world. Traditionally Malaysia has enjoyed significant trade and investment relations with the US, Japan, UK, Singapore and now China. Similar relations with other countries both Islamic and non Islamic are becoming significant, as the world globalizes.

22. We seek a quality progression. An important aspect of economic development in the Muslim credo is economic well being. One of the basic concerns of the Islamic way of life is human welfare. Economic prosperity requires most of all that we ensure the basic needs of food, shelter, clothing, and medicine are met, and essential services like water and electricity are provided. A first priority is to help the poor climb out of the pit of poverty.

23. Our political system is derived from not only the western concept of democracy but also the guidance of the Prophet (PBUH) who introduced the system of *shura*, a system of administration and style of governing based on consultation. The practice recognizes the rule of law, prizes transparency and accountability - by which the highest expression is accountability to God and to the Ummah.

24. If we follow the great tradition set during the heyday of Islamic civilization, we will seek a performance culture based on learning, scholarship and a thirst for knowledge. Except that today this can be greatly facilitated by modem multimedia and communications. There is

no need for widespread intellectual bankruptcy in this Information Age, with its emerging ethos of openness and transparency, and knowledge being accessible at the touch of a button.

25. One, of our greatest assets is our human resources - our human capital. They are our young; eager, thirsty for knowledge, skilled and trainable. Over 50% of our people are under 25 years of age - with a refreshing new Generation X approach to modem life. To realize the tremendous potential in these assets the key instrument is education. The changing scenario of science and technology requires a response. The first step is to empower our people. If we go back to the origins of Islamic decline we find that a progressive education was the main casualty. Some scholars of the time mistakenly equated learning with a narrowly defined and exclusive concept of religious knowledge. As the frontiers and scope of science expanded - sometimes astronomically, so the frontiers of knowledge expanded in tandem. Ironically the Muslim view of what is learning and scholarship shrank, dimming our vision and sapping our entrepreneurial vigor. The Islamic way of life cannot be compartmentalized into spiritual and material.

26. The perennial debate will be between religious and secular education. We still have to contend with a throw back to the doctrinaire approach. In this part of the world, we have had Islamic private education for more than 100 years from prestigious institutions to dilapidated huts where religious fervor often makes up for the lack of facilities. When Islamic religious schools are being exploited for political agendas, they may provide a breeding ground for the birth of militant and extremist behavior. Education programs - secular or religious, public or private - should be focused on quality. In this era of information and communications technology, curricula must be formulated to fulfill the demands of the times. Religious education must not deprive its learners of relevant knowledge. Oftentimes, doctrinaire religious schools fail to furnish their pupils with pertinent and applicable knowledge resulting in school-leavers finding themselves extraneous in the marketplace. Frustrated, they blame the world for not appreciating their qualities. Unfulfilled, they become easy recruits into extremism. No one needs

to be denied their religious instruction which can be accommodated separately for Muslim students in the secular system. Just as religious schools must accommodate contemporary knowledge.

27. The Muslim world must allocate greater priority and resources to its educational needs as the major drivers of economic growth in this era of knowledge, technology and innovation. It is people who steer knowledge-based economies. The transformation of commodity-based economies into knowledge based economies requires the commitment of governments and all other stakeholders to place relevant education and up-to-date skills training at the apex of national development agendas.

28. In the category of well being we should place gender equality. The stereotyped view that Islam universally oppresses women can be dispelled. It is categorically in contradiction of the Quran. The Quran places great emphasis on human dignity and freedom, therefore it is inconceivable to believe that Islam would advocate and tolerate discrimination based on ethnicity, color and gender. From ancient times, Islam has affirmed the equality and rights of women which modern nations have, only recently conceded out of social pressure. The Quran has also dedicated the Surah AI-Nisa (*An-Nisa*) specifically to women- their roles and rights. Likewise, the Prophet Muhammad (PBUH) in his last. Sermon emphasized the equality of women when he counseled, *"Treat your women well and be kind to them for they are your partners and committed helpers."* I would translate this to mean that men are not above women, neither are women above men. Rather we are equal in standing, working in partnership together using our different God-given talents, and abilities to complement each other for the glory of Allah. Treating women as second class citizens only suppresses fifty percent of our human resources and stunts the development of our countries.

29. Furthermore, when speaking about the status of women in Islam, in the eyes of Allah, the Creator of mankind and the universe, neither gender, position, intelligence, strength or beauty matter - only *taqwa* [1].

---

[1] Taqwa's meaning is fear, clinging to obedience to Allah and abandoning disobedience to Him. It is the sum of all good.

30. Islam today needs to be demonstrated intellectually as well as ritually to regain the Muslim ground. We cannot by-pass the route the West followed in the basic sciences and technology. In our case it will take a quantum leap to catch up. Taking the example of Malaysia's *Hadhari* or civilizational Islam, the national religion strives for a more, contemporary orientation. We need to embrace modernity.

31. But we find some Muslim countries lagging behind in the emerging E-world of internet usage and computer literacy. Our tech savvy young often put us to shame but there are not yet enough of them. We need to invest more on education but to invest wisely in terms of quality and relevance. Japan has 1,200 universities, 120 in or around Tokyo. Yet there are only 550 universities in 55 Muslim countries.[2]

32. In a recent survey by the Times Educational Supplement [3], ranking the best universities in global terms, American institutions occupied most of the top 10 places. In this part of the world, Beijing (17) and Singapore (18) came out best. Muslim countries were way behind.

33. The fall out is predictable. We often suffer a brain drain of our best talent. The young are impatient - will not stay if there are no opportunities for their capabilities - or no access to new skills.

34. This has a much wider connotation; economic development is about the development of man himself. In the Muslim context we instill skill and integrity. Skill is a product of education and knowledge leading to the development of entrepreneurs and innovation, the focus of the development effort. Integrity is what underpins and inspires whatever capability level we reach, in terms of high moral standards. In our sense this means Islamic tenets of integrity and justice. The eternal verities.

---

[2] Dr Mohd Ghazali bin Mohd Nor, head of the Islamic Development Bank Jeddah

[3] The Times World University Rankings, November 5th 2004

CONCLUSION

35.   Economic development, human and intellectual growth, empowerment individually and nationally, political and social stability are not achieved overnight. The Prophet (PBUH) with the guidance of Allah took 23 years to fully establish a mature system of government in Medina. Malaysia's NEP was a 20 year policy introduced in 1970 but still with us in modified form. Now we have Vision 2020 a 30-year policy to guide us towards achieving the status of a fully developed society. In all, Malaysia set aside 50 years to achieve social and economic transformation.

36. But the process may now be accelerated. The centre of gravity in the world's economic development is shifting inexorably from West to East.

37. The countries that face each other across the Pacific especially the Asia Pacific countries will become the Club of the Future with S E Asia an important Muslim enclave. Our countries must grasp the nettle - to accomplish the necessary change and adopt a strategy of development for a globalized world.

38. This predicates a belief in the future and in the infinite possibilities of technology. Muslims whose lives are predicated on belief in God are best prepared for the essential element of faith that will be required. I'd like to end with a story.

39. In 1870 in Indiana the Methodists were holding a Conference (You see they had them in those days too and this one like ours was related to a religion). The Bishop presided. A scientist got up and predicted that one day men would fly through the air like birds. The Bishop was outraged. This was heresy. In the bible, flight was reserved for the angels. He stormed out.

40. The good Bishop whose name was Wright went home to his two small sons, Orville and Wilbur.

41. We too must look to our younger generation who are not afraid of technology, in fact are excited by it to bring us to the next phase in human civilization which will supersede the Industrial Revolution and bring human kind to greater heights. This time the Muslim Ummah will share fully in the coming transformation.

42. It will require faith of the kind the good Bishop lacked but which the young Orville and Wilbur Wright possessed, and the spirit of adventure to go with it.

43. The one attribute in an increasingly godless world, which Muslims have, is their enduring faith and their moral compass.

From Saints to the Taliban: The Transformation of the Madrasah

by
Nazeer Ahmed, Ph.D.

From Saints to the Taliban:
The Transformation of the Madarash

by Nazeer Ahmed, Ph.D.

1.0. Introduction

*T*he post 9-11 climate in the world is characterized by anti-Western sentiment growing in tandem with "Islamic" extremism across the Muslim world. Terrorism, bred by a complex set of political and social conditions, has become one of the foremost challenges to global stability. While there are historical reasons for the growth of extremism, very little effort has been expended in understanding these historical roots so that the lessons learned can help plan for the future.

The madrasah is at the center of the debate surrounding the rise of extremism. The traditional educational systems in Islamic countries are suspected of having become nurseries for religious radicalism. A study of the madrasah, its history and its evolution, as well as the tensions that it faces in the modern world, take on added importance in the context of the growing perception that it is connected to the rising tide of extremism.

This paper is based on ongoing research into the correspondence between the madrasah and the historical archetypes that the Islamic civilization has produced over the centuries. These archetypes capture the functional aspirations of a society much as architecture captures its spiritual longings. That Osama bin Laden has emerged as the role model for some youth in the Islamic world is no accident. It is a result of the historical choices made by the Muslims themselves. And the madrasah, as the nursery for religious education and the cradle for religious teachers is central to this internal dialectic.

2.0. HISTORICAL PERSPECTIVES

As we scan the fourteen centuries of Islamic history, we can decipher at least seven periods when the process of education in Muslim societies went through a transformation. Each of these periods represents a noticeable "bend", an identifiable change in the direction of Islamic civilization.

The development of formal teaching in Islamic societies is embedded in the historical experience of the community. Immediately after the death of the Prophet Muhammed, people who had not known him in person flocked to his companions in search of knowledge. The structure of instruction was the halqa (study circle) and the syllabus was the prophetic knowledge. This was the age of the spiritual giants. Out of the early halqas came the great jurists like Abu Haneefa and spiritual masters like Rabia al Adawiya

The character of the madrasah went through its first transformation with the advent of the Abbasids. As the empire expanded, Greek rationalism, Indian mathematics and Persian philosophy entered the Islamic domains and challenged Arab dogma. The Muslims sought to amalgamate the knowledge they received from other civilizations with their own religious tradition. A school of translation, the Darul Hikmah was established in Baghdad. The works of Aristotle and Aryabhatta became available to the Muslims.

The Mu'tazalites who led this intellectual charge found favor with the Caliphs and guided the ship of Islam for almost a hundred years (765-846). The educational system reflected the rational bend of the age, and the syllabus included philosophy, mathematics and logic in addition to the traditional subjects.

As rationalists, the Mu'tazalites applied deductive logic to the transcendence of God and in the process, got entangled in religious controversies. The al-Hakims (integrators) emerged when the rationalists lost out. This was the "golden age" of science in Islam (800-1200) and its archetypes included Al Baruni, Omar Khayyam, and Ibn Sina. The syllabus of the age embraced the deductive as well as inductive sciences. The al-Hakims dominated the historical landscape until the devastations of the Mongols (1219-1258).

The Sufis emerged out of the ashes of the Mongol destructions. The madrasah reflected the spiritual quest of this era and the science of tazkiya (purification of the soul) found an honorable place along side religious studies. Representing the archetypes of the age were Abdel Qader Jeelani of Iraq, Mevlana Rumi of Turkey, and Shaykh Maqdum of Indonesia.

The age of the Sufis culminated in a culture of akhlaq (ethics) personified by the Great Moguls of India (1526-1707). The liberal, comprehensive curriculum of the age, and the cosmopolitan characters produced by it reflected the akhlaqi color.

As corruption ran amuck in the body politic, the salafis (puritans) asserted themselves (1650-1800). This was the beginning of the age of fatwa (legal edicts). Personifying this archetype were Abdul Wahhab of Arabia and Dan Fuduye of West Africa. In their zeal to purge the society of religious excesses, the salafis indulged in their own excesses, and injected rigidity into the educational process.

It wasn't until the nineteenth century, with European ascendancy firmly established, that the Muslims woke up to the challenge of the West. In the Ottoman Empire, this awakening resulted in a series of reforms, called the Tanzeemat. As the Ottoman Empire disintegrated, the modernists emerged. Kemal Ataturk was its archetype.

Summarily, there are distinct and identifiable breaks in Islamic history when one societal archetype disappears and a new one appears. In the emergence of these archetypes the madrasah and the instructional eco-system played a decisive role. When the syllabus and instruction were balanced and included the natural sciences, the sciences of man and the sciences of the soul (the stable nature-history-soul tripod),

Islamic civilization thrived and contributed to world civilization. When education was marginalized to one discipline or the other, it withered. Where it once produced intellectual giants it now crafted statues without spirit, bodies without soul.

It appears that Islamic civilization took a detour from taqwa (divine consciousness) to fatwa (jurisprudence), from an emphasis on spirituality to a penchant for legal edicts and the role played by the madrasah in this transformation. The consequence of this detour has been the rise to prominence of a religious fringe bereft of spirituality. The result is the rise of extremism, intolerance and violence in parts of the Islamic world.

3.0. Modern Perspectives

In modern times, the madrasah has been subjected to additional tensions. Wahhabism has made major inroads into the educational processes with a massive investment of funds. Women's education has been completely marginalized. The graduates of the madrasahs, with no skills to compete in the increasingly technological global economy, drift into the arms of the extremists, blaming all of their misfortunes on the outside world.

The madrasah is not a monolithic institution with a single structure. It appears in many shapes and forms. It has a variety of structures, and is subject to the same social and political pressures as is the society at large. It defies simplistic packaging for ten second sound bites or TV infomercials. In the context of Southeast Asia, it is at once a source for social stability and a legitimate target for cultural and political reform.

In its early years, the madrasah was a mosque-based religious institution similar to a Bible school attached to a church. It is only in recent years that the paradigm has shifted to secular education with a heavy emphasis on technical subjects.

No reliable statistics exist on the number of madrasahs in different regions of the world. Across the Islamic world, the landscape is dotted with thousands, perhaps tens of thousands of Islamic religious schools. In some areas, such as Afghanistan, they are the sole means of education for children. Some are no more than an assembly in the open, under a tree, where poor children sit on bare soil and memorize their lessons. A few are richly endowed, with millions of dollars in property, and modern facilities. All of them call themselves "deeni madrasahs" to ensure that the attendees, and the donors, know that they are different from the secular schools, and that they cater to "deen" [religion] as opposed to "duniya" [material/secular].

These madrasahs provide a valuable social service in parts of the Islamic world. In some villages, notably in the NW frontier province of Pakistan and in Afghanistan, they make the difference between literacy and illiteracy. The molvi sahib, who heads up the madrasah, teaches reading and writing in the local language, introduces the child to elementary Arabic, and facilitates basic memorization of the Qur'an and Hadith. These madrasahs around the globe -and the pesentrens in Indonesia -provide employment to scores of religious teachers who would otherwise be unemployed.

The disservice that the madrasahs perform is not in what they teach but in what they do not teach. Where it once exposed the student to a broad spectrum of disciplines, the modern madrasah limits a student to rote learning of a few subjects. Often absent is a study of natural science, mathematics, sociology or history. Gone also is tasawwuf, the spiritual dimension of Islam. So the product of a madrasah has little understanding of the modern world, feels marginalized and is alienated from it. This feeling of alienation is often reflected in the extreme positions that some mullahs take on modern issues. Such extreme positions are often transmitted to the captive audiences that the mullahs command at religious and social gatherings.

3.1. THE STUDENT BODY

The great majority of students who attend the madrasah are from the poorer sections of society. Education is closely related to cultural values.

The madrasah students come from families where the culture does not value education. Fathers who cannot afford the cost of a secular education bring their children to the madrasah so that the child gets at least an elementary education in the religious disciplines.

In recent years, the influx of middle class Muslims into the Tableeghi Jamaat has worked to the benefit of the madrasahs, as the Jamaat prefers religious schools to secular ones. The escapist orientation of the Tableeghi Jamaat and the deeni (as opposed to dunaywi) orientation of these schools tend to complement each other. Consequently, the economic profile of a typical student in a madrasah has somewhat improved.

In addition to imparting elementary education (taalim), the madrasah performs a secondary function, that of tarbiyat. In practice, this second function is even more important than the first. Tarbiyat means molding of character. In the same sense that a potter molds a pot on a wheel, the teacher in a madrasah molds a pupil. Discipline tends to be very strict, indeed harsh, in most madrasahs. The tarbiyat function of a madrasah is what distinguishes a religious school from a secular school. Whether a graduate of a madrasah becomes an extremist or a Sufi depends on the tarbiyat that the molvi or the shaikh imparts to the student.

The dropout rate in most madrasahs is high. Sometimes it is as high as 60 percent. This could be attributed in part to the underlying poverty of the families and partly to the harsh discipline imposed on the students. Grinding poverty compels many a promising teenager to quit school and enter the work force to support the family. Those who complete a few years of schooling seek employment as mullahs in small villages where incomes are low and opportunities few. Those who complete their diploma and earn the degree of a'lim, have their horizons on larger and greener pastures in the towns and cities where there is more money and the opportunity to build lucrative trusts is much higher.

3.2. Impact of Colonialism

The colonial period introduced a historical discontinuity into the evolution of the madrasah. The injection of foreign and alien interference scuttled the natural evolution of this institution. The discontinuity may be illustrated by examining the syllabus followed before and after the colonial period. We have summarized in the next paragraph the syllabus as it was during the period of the Great Mogul Akbar (circa 1600) and as it is today.

According to Abdul Hasnat Nadvi (10), the syllabus during the Mogul period in India included the study of akhlaq (good character), arithmetic, astronomy, tareeq (history), mantiq (grammar), tib (medicine), falahat (public good), masahat (equality), hindsa (geometry), languages (Arabic, Farsi), literature, tazkiya (purification of the soul), tadbeer (planning), manzil (goal setting), ramal (management), siasat e madani (city politics), ilahiyat (theology), Qur'an, Hifz and Hadith. By contrast, today's madrasahs teach only the Qur'an, Hifz, Hadith, languages, ilahiyat and the most elementary arithmetic.

The colonial authorities were interested in training clerks for their vast colonial administrative machineries. Subjects such as mathematics and science that were not related to the administrative functions were discouraged and abandoned. The situation has persisted to this day in most madrasahs.

The marginalized syllabus of the madrasah produces graduates who are not equipped to compete in the emerging global economy. Frustrated and disillusioned, they walk into the arms of the extremists who blame all their misfortunes on the outside world.

3.3. The Influence of Wahhabism

Over the last forty years, there has been a steady and substantial flow of funds from Saudi Arabia and the Gulf into the madrasahs of the world. This inflow has been a mixed blessing. Money taints the natural growth of culture much in the same way as foreign political dominance. While oil money did help build the infrastructure of some schools, the price paid was the abandonment of the spiritual Islam that had grown up in much of the world over a thousand years, and its replacement by a largely ritualistic, puritanical Islam that is the hallmark of Wahhabism. The result is the growth of a religious edifice without soul. Into this spiritual vacuum the extremists have walked in, hoisting their political agendas, and causing mayhem around the world.

This paradigm is beginning to change. Successive wars have drained the resources of the Gulf countries. More recently, after 9/11, with "terrorism" becoming a household world, many governments have clamped down on the international transfer of funds. These developments have placed a financial crunch on the madrasahs. With sources of foreign funds drying up, the madrasahs have had to fall back on local resources.

Notwithstanding the decreasing external financial support, many madrasahs around the globe continue to look to the Saudi universities for guidance on their curriculum. The influence of Wahhabism continues to be strong with or without external financial support.

3.4. EDUCATION OF WOMEN

Historically, separate schools have existed in Islamic societies for the education of women. The celebrated ninth century Sufi master, Rabia al Adawiya of Basrah is known to have taught both men and women. As Islam found a home in Asia and Africa, the tradition of providing education to women continued.

However, in recent years, the education of women has been neglected. Grinding poverty, social inertia, and the strict segregation of women imposed by extremist elements, have all taken their toll. In Kashmir, for instance, illiteracy among women runs over seventy percent. In Afghanistan, women's schools were shut down by the Taliban. In the face of such widespread illiteracy, any discussion of the rights of women would be meaningless. This area must receive the first priority during any reformation efforts.

3.5. TECHNOLOGY & THE MADRASAH

Science and technology have had a checkered history among Muslim people. The scientific method was cultivated by Muslim scholars in Spain and Central Asia in the Middle Ages. But it withered after the Mongol invasions of the thirteenth century. In succeeding centuries, Muslim scholars, while paying lip service to the need for mastering science and technology, looked with deep suspicion on anything that disturbed their partitioning of the sacred and the profane. The introduction of the printing press into Muslim societies is a case in point. While the printing press was introduced into Europe in the fifteenth century, it was not until 1728 that it found acceptance in the Ottoman Empire. It was introduced into Mogul India even later. The reason was the determined opposition of the ulema who felt that the Word of God, namely the Qur'an, would be defiled if it touched a wooden or iron press. While the printing press made possible the wide diffusion of books in Europe, the Muslim world remained far behind. It is not uncommon even to this day to find a mullah who proclaims that science is secular and it fosters unbelief.

But the pervasive effects of technology cannot be avoided, not even by the most insular madrasah. Technology transforms societies and cultures and the madrasah cannot escape the winds of change. In slow measure, even the most orthodox ulema have started to bend in the direction of technological education. At Madrase Baqius Salehat near Bangalore, the students learn to use computers along with memorization of the Qur'an and Hadith. Mobile phones are used by molvis to talk to each other. IT driven technologies have made the principals and the sheikhs realize the need to upgrade the teaching of science and mathematics. Before they graduate, many a school in Southern India requires their students to obtain the equivalent of a high school diploma. These changes, albeit small, are a fundamental and welcome departure from the rigidity that characterized the religious syllabus until recent times.

3.6. THE IMPACT OF 9/11

The perception has grown that the perpetrators of the 9/11 attack on the world trade center were products of madrasahs. Based on published reports, the perpetrators, most of whom came from Saudi Arabia and Egypt, were more secular than religious. As far as this writer is aware, no connection has been proven between the perpetrators and the madrasahs. Nonetheless, the accusation is repeated often times, and most people in America have come to believe, that the attack was connected with students who attend madrasahs. Indeed the madrasah has been accused of being the breeding ground for "jihadis" and "terrorists". If perception is reality, it has hurt the image of the madrasah in the global consciousness. And it will affect, fundamentally and profoundly, the further evolution of the madrasah as we go forward in the twenty first century.

There have been several consequences of this xenophobia. Money, which used to flow freely from Saudi Arabia and other Gulf countries, has decreased to a trickle. Donations from the United States and other Western nations have just about stopped. The allegations against several Islamic charities have fostered a sense of fear among potential donors. The madrasahs now must fend for themselves and depend on local support.

A much more disastrous result of 9/11 and the injection of the term "terrorism" into politics is the destruction of educational links that have existed between religious schools and seminaries in different parts of the world. For almost a millennium, the madrasahs in Southern India radiated their influence far beyond the borders of South Asia. As early as the twelfth century, the migration of Awliya [saints or learned men] from the trading communities of Southern India and Gujarat, along with scholars from the Persian Gulf, was responsible for the introduction of Islam into the Indonesian and Malaysian Archipelago. Until recently, the madrasahs in South Asia attracted students from Sri Lanka, Maldives Islands, Malaysia and Indonesia. Alumni from the schools of Vanambadi and Salem are scattered all over Southeast Asia.

Because of restrictions following 9/11 and the suspicion that the madrasah is a breeding ground for terrorists, that educational link has been cut. Now, these students come no more and an age-old connection between India and SE Asia has been broken. The movement of scholars and students and the cross-fertilization of ideas and cultures that it fostered for a thousand years has been scuttled. Student exchanges foster international understanding and are a major element in the liberalization of the madrasah. The scuttling of this process will increase the isolation and alienation of the madrasah from liberal global currents.

4.0. Initiatives for Reformation

While the issue of extremism is a complex one and its relationship to the madrasah is subject to further study, there are initiatives that the madrasahs can take to align themselves with the needs of a changing world culture.

4.1. Reformation of the Syllabus

If history is any guide, a reform process which is strongly opposed by the mullahs, is likely to fail, or cause a major social upheaval. Kemalist Turkey achieved such reforms but the Kemalist revolution was the tail end of a long series of reformations starting with the Tanzeemat in the first half of the nineteenth century. And the Kemalists had to use coercive methods to ensure that the reforms would succeed.

An attempt at the transformation of the syllabus must therefore be gradual, preserving the stability that this institution provides while enhancing its social usefulness. The changes must also come from within the community rather than imposed from the top. A first step in this direction is to reintroduce into the syllabus a study of the mathematical, natural and historical sciences as well as Qur'anic spirituality (tazkiya). These subjects were a part of the Nizamiya Nisab as late as the eighteenth century. Once mathematics is mastered, science, philosophy and the natural sciences will follow. Gradually, the Nizamiya Nisab will be transformed into an Islamic Nisab embracing the Qur'anic sciences, mathematics, the natural sciences, philosophy and technology, and will become an anchor for Islamic civilization rather than a nursery for extremists.

4.2. TEACHING METHODS

The instruction in the madrasah is characterized by rote learning. The deductive and inductive methods are totally absent. For the graduates of the madrasahs to participate and compete in the global economy, it is essential that they acquire analytical skills. Computer training is a must. Changes are required in the methods of instruction so that the students, in addition to a memorization of the Qur'an and Hadith, acquire the skills that will enable them to find jobs in the global marketplace.

4.3. TEACHER TRAINING

Teacher training is a key to the reformation process. Teacher training offers the highest potential for student reach. It provides the highest benefit-to-cost ratio. It also exposes the vast majority of pesentren teachers to the beauty and majesty of the natural and historical sciences in an Islamic framework. However, teacher training requires considerable resources and external assistance.

4.4. NGO & GOVERNMENT ASSISTANCE

A transformation of the madrasah, its syllabus and teaching methods, cannot take place without a substantial investment of funds from the outside. NGOs and government organizations can assist with the preparation of books and training material, teacher training, computer training, technical skills acquisition and job placement. NGOs can act as advocates for the madrasahs with their governments, championing the transformation of this historic institution into an asset for the construction of civil and democratic societies.

5.0. Suggested Readings

1. Ahmed, Akbar S, "Islam Today", Tauris Publications, New York, 2001.

2. Ahmed, Nazeer, "Islam in Global History", Vols. 1 and 2, Suhail Academy, Lahore, 2003.

3. Ahmed, Nazeer, "Modern Issues in Islamic Education", 5 articles, Pakistan Link, Los Angeles, August 7, 2003 to September 5, 2004.

4. "Islam and Civil Society: The Path to Transformation", International Conference of Islamic Scholars, Jakarta, Indonesia, Proceedings, December 21-24, 2004.

5. The Asia Foundation, "Educational Reform in Indonesia", IslamiCity, July 30, 2004.

6. Benard, Cheryl, "Civil Democratic Islam, Partners, Resources and Strategies", RAND Corporation, National Security Research Division, 2003.

7. Doi, Abdur Rahman, "Women in Society", Zaira, Nigeria: Ahmadu Bello University, Center for Islamic Legal Studies, 2001

8. Fuad, Muhammad, "Civil Society in Indonesia: The Potential and Limits of Muhammadiyah", J. of Social Issues in Southeast Asia, Vol. 17, October 2002, pp. 133-136.

9. Iqbal, Mohammed, "The Reconstruction of Religious Thought in Islam", Adam Publishers, New Delhi, 1997.

10. Nadvi, Syed Abul Hasan, "Hindustan ki purani darsgarahen" (Ancient madrasahs in Hindustan), Lahore, 1916.

11. Nasr, Seyyed Hossein, "Science and Civilization in Islam", the New American Library, 1968.

12. Wadud, Amina, "Qur'an and Woman: Rereading the Sacred Text from a Woman's Perspective", New York: Oxford University Press, 1999.

Voluntary Associations & Civic Values in Premodern Islam

by
Professor Vincent J. Cornell, Ph.D.

University of Arkansas

Voluntary Associations
& Civic Values in Premodern Islam

by Professor Vincent J. Cornell, Ph.D.

Shortly before he was killed in a gun battle with Saudi security forces in June 2003, an Al Qaeda activist named Yusuf al-Ayyeri published an essay that portrayed democracy as a grave threat to Islam. According to Ayyeri, the philosophical basis of democracy is the concept of the autonomous individual, which has been used to justify individualistic doctrines of modernity such as religious pluralism and moral relativism. The combination of democracy and individualism, Ayyeri asserted, undermines God-given moral standards by basing political relations on the lowest common denominator of human values. By denying divine governance, democracy "seductively" causes people to believe that they are the authors of their own destinies and that they can alter the laws that govern them. Muslims living in a democracy would ignore the rules that God commanded, would undermine the Shari'a as the expression of God's will, and would "love this world, forget the next world, and abandon jihad."[1] The gendered tone of Ayyeri's critique is unmistakable: Eve, in the guise of liberal democracy, seduces Adam (Islam) into accepting the forbidden fruits of moral autonomy and free will. According to Ayyeri's pessimistic moral calculus, theological and moral relativism are the inevitable consequences of liberal individualism and individualism is the ideological mask worn by egoism, the greatest sin in Islam.

In Europe and America, Ayyeri's fear of liberal democracy is mirrored by a similar fear of radical Islamic values. Recently, Theo Van Gogh, a Dutch filmmaker who produced a deliberately insulting film that ridiculed Muslim attitudes toward women, was killed and nearly decapitated by a Dutch-Moroccan avenger of Islam. Ayaan Hirsi Ali, a feminist activist and former Muslim of Somali origin, was threatened in a letter found attached to Van Gogh's body. She is now in hiding

---

[1] Amir Taheri, "Al-Qaeda's Agenda for Iraq," *New York Post Online Edition*, September 4, 2003.

and has been unable to occupy her seat in the Dutch Parliament. At a recent seminar at the Brookings Institution, Francis Fukuyama, a noted American advocate of liberal democracy, claimed that "Europeans are threatened internally by radical Islam in a much more severe way than Americans are in terms of their external threat." As a way of responding to this alleged threat, Fukuyama called for an end to "the stifling political correctness" that has prevented Western democracies from more aggressively insisting on the maintenance of liberal values. "There is no way you can appease Muslim radicalism," said one participant at the conference. "If you go down that route, you will end up banning the sale of alcohol in supermarkets."[2]

To a person like myself, who lives in a southern American state where the sale of alcohol is already banned in supermarkets and where liquor stores must be located at least six blocks away from a school, this is hardly a world-shaking problem. However, the fears about social and political values expressed by Al Qaeda ideologues such as Ayyeri and right-wing liberal democrats such as Fukuyama, although excessive, should not be dismissed out of hand. The totalitarian nature of many Islamist political movements would in fact make it difficult to establish a democratic political culture in some Muslim countries. Conversely, liberal notions of moral autonomy and free will may indeed pose a threat to traditional ways of Muslim life, if not to Islam itself. Ironically, the critiques of Western philosophy and political culture expressed by Al Qaeda activists are at times more clearly attuned to actual value conflicts than are the defenses of democracy mounted by Islamic liberals and other Muslim apologists for modernity. To say, for example, that Ayman al-Zawahiri is a more perceptive critic of Western political culture than Tariq Ramadan is like saying that the Marquis de Sade was a more perceptive critic of morality than Voltaire. For all that we may despise of Zawahiri's and de Sade's conclusions, we must at times admit that the logic of their arguments is sound. If it proves nothing else, the extremism of Zawahiri and de Sade shows us that one can be logically correct and morally wrong at the same time.

---

[2] "Charlemagne: A civil war on terrorism," *The Economist*, Volume 373 Number 8403, November 27th-December 3rd 2004, 56.

Figures such as Zawahiri and de Sade also remind us that if the case is to be made for a democratic reform of Islam, it must be based on arguments that are superior to those of the extremists. Such arguments must be authentically rooted in the intellectual traditions of premodern Islam, but must also allow for interaction between Islamic scriptures and the interpretive processes of the present. The Qur'an can only display the fullness of its message when a variety of interpretive methods are allowed. But allowing for a wider range of textual reasoning is not enough by itself. The argument for democracy in Islam must also be based on a thorough understanding of liberal philosophy, a comprehensive knowledge of the varieties of democratic forms in the West, and a critical and historical understanding not only of Islamic ideals, but also of the successes and failures of Muslims who have tried to put those ideals into practice. So far, contemporary Muslim thought has not measured up to this task. The present paper is an attempt to show how such a post-liberal inquiry might proceed.

WHAT IS CIVIL SOCIETY?

Before assessing the precedents for civil society in Islam, we must first understand what the term means in the West. Although there are a variety of approaches to the concept, two of these approaches have been particularly influential. In the United States, the notion of civil society is based on a "bottom-up" or democratic pluralist view of civic organization. According to this view, to use the words of Alexis de Tocqueville in *Democracy in America* (ca. 1835-40), "The people reign over the political world as God reigns over the universe."[3] For Tocqueville, as for all classic theorists of liberal democracy, popular sovereignty is exercised through self-government, which promotes the common good by expressing the will of the majority.[4] A democratic pragmatist such as John Dewey (d. 1952) might add that a desire for self-government and a concern for the common good are not inborn

---

[3] Alexis de Tocqueville, *Democracy in America* (New York: Doubleday Anchor Books, 1969), 60.

[4] See Frank Cunningham, *Theories of Democracy: A Critical Introduction* (London: Routledge, 2002), 9-12.

values, but depend on education and experience. In the United States, democratic values were nurtured by a political culture of engagement that developed out of local voluntary associations where citizens of similar social standing, education, and temperament practiced the skills of self-rule. This view of civil society was affirmed by Thomas Jefferson (d. 1826) in an 1820 letter when he wrote: "I know no safe depository of the ultimate powers of the society but the people themselves; and if we think them not enlightened enough to exercise their control with a wholesome discretion, the remedy is not to take it from them, but to inform their discretion by education."[5]   On the view put forth by Jefferson, Tocqueville, and Dewey, "civil society" refers to all associations, whether governmental or non-governmental, that act as incubators for the development of democratic self-government. The aims of civil society are to promote the general interest over individual interests, and to respect and protect the right of individual expression. Thus, to truly fit the American model of civil society, civil society in Islam must meet two fundamental requirements: it must promote the general interest over parochial interests, and it must allow for dissenting views.

In a recent study of democracy in Italy, Robert Putnam reaffirmed this view of civil society by finding that democracy works best under the following conditions: 1) when citizens participate actively in public affairs; 2) when citizens participate in society as social equals; 3) when citizens interact with each other on the basis of mutual trust and respect. Putnam found these conditions to prevail most fully when citizens are active participants in voluntary associations such as sport clubs, cooperatives, mutual aid societies, cultural associations, and voluntary unions. According to Putnam, participation in such organizations creates "social capital"— a reservoir of trust and commitment to common purposes that is necessary for civil society to exist.[6] The virtue of democracy is that it is the most effective means of investing such social capital. However, the mere fact that voluntary associations such

---

[5]   Letter to William Charles Jarvis, 28 September 1820, in P. L. Ford (ed.) *Writings of Thomas Jefferson* vol. 10 (1899), 161.

[6]   Cunningham, *Theories of Democracy, 23-24. See also, Robert Putnam, Making Democracy Work: Civic Traditions in Modern Italy* (Princeton, New Jersey: Princeton University Press, 1993).

as those studied by Putnam are independent from the state should not be taken to mean that civil society always stands in opposition to the state. On the contrary, according to the American model of civil society, voluntary associations act as training sites for democratic participation in all contexts, including government and the state. Another key, then, to the understanding of civil society in the United States is that voluntary associations can be a means of building up social capital.

By contrast, notions of civil society in France and many Francophone countries are based on a "top-down" model that comes from the theories of Jean-Jacques Rousseau (d. 1778). Rousseau was less concerned with promoting democracy per se than with promoting the "General Will." He saw the General Will as expressed through a "body politic" that is constituted through a free and equal association of citizens and held together by the desire of citizens to promote the common good.[7] This association of citizens is regulated by a social contract that symbolizes the General Will. What is "free" in such associations is the attempt by citizens, conceived equally and without regard for social status, to create a contract that promotes the common good. Once the social contract is agreed upon, however, there is no provision in Rousseau's theory to guarantee that the association thus created must follow democratic procedures. All that is necessary is that civil society promotes the General Will. It is thus much easier to find potential Islamic precedents for civil society on the Rousseauian model than on the liberal democratic model advocated by American thinkers, because for Rousseau, the voluntary associations that constitute civil society do not have to promote democratic self-government.

Rousseau agreed with his American counterparts that civil society and the state are not necessarily rivals. In fact, the state may be the best expression of civil society. When a state expresses the General Will by identifying itself with the body politic, there is no need for civil society to be separate from the state, because state and civil society are more or less the same. Although it reflects the values of participatory democracy in its formative stages, Rousseau's social contract can potentially become

---

[7] Cunningham, *Theories of Democracy*, 124

a totalitarian concept. Within the Body Politic, the rulers and the ruled are one. Thus, the interests of the state and its citizens are likely to coincide: "The better the constitution of a State is, the more do public affairs encroach on private in the minds of the citizens," claimed Rousseau.[8]   In other words, as long as the state reflects the General Will, it makes little difference whether the government or independent associations create social welfare organizations, syndicates, NGOs, and the like; in either case such organizations are part of civil society. In fact, Rousseau would most likely say that state-supported civic associations better express the General Will than do independent associations. This is because independent associations might undermine the social contract by promoting not the General Will, but what Rousseau called the Will of All— the atomistic and disunited sum of self-interested personal wills.

The idealistic notion of civil society promoted by Rousseau is significantly different from the more pragmatic notion of civil society promoted by Jefferson and his successors. In this regard, it is important to note that contemporary models of civil society in the Islamic world have more in common with the French version than with the American. In part, this is because Rousseau's model of civil society expresses the concept of participatory democracy rather than liberal democracy as a political ideal. Prior to recent democratic developments in Malaysia, Indonesia, Turkey, and now Afghanistan, most democratic initiatives in the Muslim world were participatory rather than liberal-democratic. In addition, Rousseau's idealism and unitary perspective recall certain Islamic models of government such as Ibn Taymiyya's theory of Divine Governance (*al-siyasa al-shar'iyya*). Like Rousseau, Ibn Taymiyya promoted the ideal of social unity, although in his case it was based on the theological unity of tawhid rather than on a secular social contract. It should come as no surprise, therefore, that Islamic political movements that advocate the so-called "Tawhidic" perspective are more likely to turn to Rousseau than to Jefferson for models of government and civil society. But that is the subject of another paper. What is important to note at the present juncture is that voluntary associations in premodern

---

[8] Ibid, 127, quoting from Rousseau, *The Social Contract*.

Islam have no *a priori* connection with either of these two Western models of civil society.

State and Society in Premodern Islam

One of the reasons why premodern voluntary associations in Islam cannot be directly incorporated into modern notions of civil society is that premodern Muslims were not "citizens" in the present sense of the word. The identity of the modern citizen is dependent on the idea of the nation-state: it is bound up with notions of a common homeland, a common territory, a common government, a common language, common customs, a common religion, and a sense of social union that reflects common values.[9] The idea of nationhood is also reinforced by symbolic tokens such as a flag, diplomatic recognition, a national army, and membership in international bodies such as the United Nations. In modern nation-states, civil society institutions are seen to play an important role in the development of national unity.

The juridical scholars who wrote theoretical critiques of the state in premodern Islam had no notion of nationhood or citizenship. The associations that they belonged to were both wider and more parochial than the modern nation. A scholar from Beirut could not call himself "Lebanese," for example, because there was no nation of Lebanon. He could assert his identity as a Sunni or Shiite Muslim, but such an identity was confessional rather than national. Apart from his Islamic and sectarian identities, the primary loyalties of a premodern Muslim scholar could be deduced almost entirely from the relationships expressed in his name. His sense of homeland was limited to the locale in which he was born and his personal loyalties were defined for the most part by tribal or familial ties of kinship. As for the wider, religious and intellectual values that Muslim scholars upheld, these were universal values, not national values.

---

[9] For a thorough discussion of the ideology of nationhood, see Benedict Anderson, *Imagined Communities: Reflections of the Origin and Spread of Nationalism* (London and New York: Verso, revised edition 1991).

In particular, the independent Muslim scholar went to great lengths to avoid identifying himself with the state. Most states in the premodern Islamic world were coercive enterprises that amounted to protection rackets. The Arabic term, *sultan*, means "one who exercises power (*sulta*)," or in more colloquial terms, "strongman" or "dictator." Sultans and their officials ruled over a populace that was designated as *al-ra'iya*, "the Flock." A flock of sheep is cared for only because it is a source of profit. Just as a flock of sheep needs a shepherd and a sheep dog, the political Flock needed the ruler and his army for protection against local unrest and external invasion. In return for this protection, the Flock paid taxes that supported the ruler and his army and legitimized the use of force. This relationship was expressed in a formula known as the "Circle of Equity." This formula, which owed its origin to the Seljuk Turks who ruled over Central Asia, Iran, and Iraq in the eleventh and twelfth centuries CE, expressed the relationship between the Flock, the ruler, and his army in the following way:

1. There can be no authority without the military.

2. There can be no military without wealth.

3. The Flock produces the wealth.

4. The Sultan cares for the Flock by promoting justice.

5. Justice requires harmony in the world.

6. The world is a garden and its walls are the state.

7. The support of the state is the *Shari'a*.

8. There is no support for the *Shari'a* without the military.[10]

Apologists for the state used the arguments of physical protection and defense of the *Shari'a* as their main strategies of justification. However, despite the apparent logic of the Circle of Equity, the fact was that the most common threat to the general interest was the state itself. Although medieval Muslim jurists often complained about the

---

[10] Norman Itzkowitz, *Ottoman Empire and Islamic Tradition* (Chicago, 1972), 88.

exploitative nature of the state, the basic premises of the system were seldom challenged. Muslim jurists had a deep and abiding fear of social unrest (*fitna*). For them, any government was better than anarchy, so long as internal security was maintained and state exploitation was not so excessive as to create social unrest itself. Numerous examples of the exploitative nature of the state can be found in books of Islamic law (*fiqh*) where the expropriation of property (*ghasb*) by the state was a major subject of discussion.[11] The difference between "Islamic" and "un-Islamic" forms of taxation was also an important source of concern. Although jurists sometimes stood up against the state in the interest of the general welfare, the danger of this option made it rare. Effective protection (i.e., protection from the "protectors") was most often secured by relying on alternate networks of power, such as those of kin and tribe, or powerful individuals such as Sufi saints.

Justice as Fair Proportion. Because of the nature of the state and the tensions it produced, many of the associations that approximated civil society in premodern Islam were devoted to the promotion of justice. The culture of justice in the medieval Islamic world was more about proportion than equality. The root meaning of *'adl*, the Arabic word for "justice," does not connote "equality," as in sameness, but rather conveys the idea of fairness, in the sense of "restoring balance." It has much in common with the Greek word for justice, *dikaiosune*, which also connotes fairness rather than equality.[12] This was understood by Muslim jurists and theologians, who recognized in *'adl* and the related term *haqq* Aristotle's notion of distributive justice. Aristotle defined justice in terms of the mean: "To do injustice is to have more than one ought, and to suffer it is to have less than one ought."[13] Corrective

---

[11] See, for example, Abu al'Abbas Ahmad ibn Yahya al-Wansharisi (d. 1508), *al-Mi'yar al-mu'rib wa al-jami' al-mughrib 'an fatawi ahl Ifriqiyya wa al-Andalus wa al-Maghrib* (Rabat, 1981), vol. 9, 537-582, "Decisions Concerning Usurpation (*ghasb*), Compulsion (*ikrah*), and Proprietary Rights (*istihqaq*)." The subject of rape (*ightisab*) is also included in this section.

[12] Alasdair MacIntyre, *A Short History of Ethics: A History of Moral Philosophy from the Homeric Age to the Twentieth Century* (Notre Dame, Indiana, 1998), 11. For Aristotle, distributive justice was a matter of ratios. See idem, *Nicomachean Ethics*, translated by Martin Oswald (Indianapolis, Indiana, 1962), pp. 118-128. Aristotle also believed that "In justice, every virtue is summed up," and that "Ruling will show the man" (Ibid, 114).

[13] MacIntyre, *A Short History of Ethics*, 79.

justice entails restoring the fair proportion that has been lost. This corresponds to the Arabic term *haqq*, which means "right" (in the sense of personal or legal rights), "law," "truth," or "portion." To be a just man in premodern Islam meant to uphold the right (*haqq*), which is the ethical aspect of divine truth (*haqq*). When a person commits an injustice, he or she must reestablish the mean by restoring things to their original nature (*haqiqa*). This is accomplished by reaffirming (*tahaqquq*) the proper distribution of goods so that everyone receives his rightful share (*haqq*).

When justice is conceived as fair proportion, receiving ones rightful share does not mean receiving the same as everyone else. Society in premodern Islam was assumed to be hierarchical, so distributing goods equally would mean that some people would receive more than their natural right, thus creating a new injustice. Medieval Muslim societies were not democracies. But they were not caste systems either, and it was possible for a bright peasant or one of the urban poor to become a scholar, a Sufi saint, or even a notable. However, the typical peasant was not a notable, and did not expect to be treated like one. Islamic legal notions of distributive justice did not advocate social revolutions that might upset the just mean. The scholars and Sufis who were social reformers may have spoken for the people, but they almost never called for "power to the people."

A good illustration of the notion of justice as fair proportion can be found in the biography of the Moroccan Sufi Abu al-'Abbas al-Sabti (d. 1204), the patron saint of the city of Marrakech. In his role as patron and spokesman for the poor of Marrakech, the entirety of Sabti's career was based on the notion of distributive justice. The systematic way in which Sabti distributed the donations that came into his hands is one of the clearest expressions of proportional ethics to be found anywhere:

> I divide everything that comes to me into seven portions. I take one-seventh for myself and the second-seventh for that which I am required to spend on my wife and the small children under her care, as well as the slaves and slave-girls, all of whom

number thirty-two individuals. Then I look after those who have lost their sustenance; they are the neglected orphans who have neither mother nor father. I take them in as my own family and see to it that not one of them lacks a marriage or a funeral, unless someone else provides it for them. Then I look after my kinfolk, who number eighty-four individuals. They have two rights: their right as family members and their right as residents [in my household]. Then come those who have been deprived of their support as mentioned in the Book of God Most High. They are the poor who have fallen into hardship on the Way of God—those who are unable to work the land and are thought of as ignorant, but who are rich in patience and restraint; they are the ones unable to manage their own affairs. I take them in as if they are my own relatives, and when one of them dies, I replace him with another.[14]

At the height of his career, Sabti presided over a charitable organization that was comparable to that established by Mother Theresa in Calcutta. The saint who had formerly lived alone in a cave outside of Marrakech now resided in a large house near the Kutubiyya mosque, and the Almohad Sultan of Morocco personally maintained a hostel and a madrasa for his disciples. Sabti's Sufi-run charitable enterprise was the largest voluntary association in the Almohad capital.

A similar institution was maintained in the Middle Atlas Mountains of Morocco by Abu Yi'zza Yalannur (d. 1177), who is revered today as the patron saint of Morocco's Berber (Amazigh) peoples. Abu Yi'zza maintained a *madrasa*, a food distribution center, and a hostel for guests. Among the miracles associated with this saint was his ability to minister to everyone according to proportional notions of distributive justice. Whenever guests came to him, he would provide a meal appropriate to their social status: a poor shepherd was likely to get a bowl of cooked barley and milk; a farmer might get couscous and vegetables; a merchant

---

[14] Vincent J. Cornell, *Realm of the Saint: Power and Authority in Moroccan Sufism* (Austin, Texas, 1998), 85. This quotation comes from Abu Ya'qub Yusuf ibn al-Zayyat al-Tadili (d. 1231), *al-Tashawwuf ila rijal al-tasawwuf wa akhbar Abi'l-'Abbas al-Sabti, Ahmed Toufiq*, ed. (Rabat, 1984), 459-461

or a scholar might get couscous, vegetables, and reconstituted dried meat (*gdid*); a prince or a high notable was likely to receive couscous with vegetables and fresh meat. However, when it came to individual acts of charity, Abu Yi'zza was more altruistic. A scholar who spent considerable time with this saint describes him as holding regularly scheduled audiences, where he would consider petitions from fellow *Imazighen* who walked barefoot for many miles through the mountains to seek his blessings and advice. Abu Yi'zza's altruism was so great that he would give up pieces of his turban, the food on his plate, and even the hairs on his head to those who desired them.[15]

Were Sabti and Abu Yi'zza consciously following Aristotle's model of distributive justice? Or were they simply carrying out the Qur'anic injunction, "Verily Allah commands justice (*'adl*), the doing of good (*ihsan*), and giving to one's near relatives" (16:90)? Most likely, it was the latter rather than the former, at least in the case of Abu Yi'zza. However, the notion of distributive justice in Islam had become so imbued with Aristotelian ethics that Aristotle's concept of justice was integral to the understanding of the Qur'an itself. Sabti's notion of corrective justice was clearly Aristotelian. His way of restoring a just balance through the redistribution of personal wealth was not aimed at social equalization, but at the restoration of a just ratio of goods, whether they were assessed in money, property, or food. Termed by Sabti "sharing in proportionate measure" (*mushatara*), this form of restitution consisted of a miraculous extortion whereby those who had "more than they ought" were compelled by threat of divine punishment to redistribute excess wealth to those who had "less than they ought." For the most part, excess wealth was redistributed to individuals. At times, however, the redistribution was collective, as when Sabti convinced the daughter of the Almohad ruler of Marrakech to donate 1,000 gold dinars for the city's poor. Sabti's saintly extortion was a powerfully symbolic way of restoring justice and teaching civic values at the same time. What ultimately protected him from the state was the fact that for Sabti, "excess" did not mean

---

[15] Cornell, *Realm of the Saint*, 70. This account comes from Muhammad ibn al-Qasim al-Tamimi, Kitab *al-mustafad fi dhikr al-salihin wa al-'ubbad bi-madinat Fas wa ma yaliha min al-bilad* (Rabat, Bibliothèque Générale, ms. 5168), 14-16.

"surplus," so he never demanded more than the just mean. Sabti was not a Moroccan Robin Hood. He did not take from the rich and transfer their wealth to the poor. His "racket," if it can be called such, was to offer the elites of Marrakech protection from God's corrective justice by indemnifying them through acts of charity. "Who is it that will give to God a goodly loan, so that He may increase it many fold?" (2:245) asks the Qur'an. Sabti, a philosophically trained scholar who was noted for his precise use of the Arabic language, expressed this principle through a popular maxim whose words he changed to make his point more effectively: "Existence (i.e., success) is actualized through generosity" (*al-wujud yanfa'ilu bi-l-jud*).[16]

Voluntary Associations and the General Will

In the Sufi tradition of North Africa, one of the earliest terms for "saint" was *salih*. This is the same term used in the phrase, *al-Salaf al-Salih*, which refers to the Prophet Muhammad's Companions and the "righteous forebears" that followed them. The Qur'an mentions the *salihin*, along with martyrs and propagators of the Islamic message, as people whom Allah has favored (4:69). A *salih* (fem. *saliha*) is a morally upstanding person who performs good deeds (*salah*) and strives for the improvement (*islah*) of oneself and others.[17] A socially conscious approach to spirituality was one of the hallmarks of Sufism in the premodern Maghrib. Often, this social consciousness was manifested in acts of charity or conflict resolution, as with Sabti and Abu Yi'zza. At other times, it was expressed in the form of a moral and educational revival. This was the case with Abu Muhammad Salih (d. 1234), whose tomb in the Moroccan coastal city of Asafi is still an important place of pilgrimage. His significance in the context of civil society formation lies in the fact that he established a yearly, Sufi-led pilgrimage caravan that was supported by an extensive network of way stations, hostels, and

---

[16] Cornell, *Realm of the Saint*, 91. The original saying is, "Existence is made better through generosity" (*al-Wujud yantafi'u bi-l-jud*).

[17] Ibid, 6.

centers for teaching that extended from Morocco to Alexandria, Cairo, Jerusalem, and the holy cities of Arabia.[18]

Abu Muhammad Salih spent nearly twenty years of his life in Alexandria. While there, he thought of using the pilgrimage to Mecca as a means of developing a greater consciousness of Islam and its teachings in the Far Maghrib. Since the Hajj pilgrimage brought together Muslims from all parts of the world, it offered a unique opportunity for believers to interact with and learn from each other. Upon returning to his home region, Abu Muhammad Salih founded a mosque and a *ribat* (teaching center) at Asafi, an ancient fishing village that was being developed as a port for the city of Marrakech. He made Ribat Asafi the headquarters of an ethnically based Sufi order, which he named *al-Ta'ifa al-Magiriyya* after his own tribe, the Banu Magir. In time, the Magiriyya became the semi-official Sufi order for the highland Masmuda Imazighen (Berbers) south of Marrakech. State officials became concerned about the political implications of the Magiriyya almost as soon as it was founded. Particularly worrisome was their use of symbolic tokens of group identity, such as shaving the head and wearing distinctive clothing. This Magiriyya "uniform" included a number of articles that were adopted from eastern Sufism, such as the patched cloak (*muraqqa'a*), staff (*'asa*), pouch (*rakwa*), and soft cap (*shashiyya*) of the brotherhoods of Iraq and eastern Iran. Another sign of group identity was a large rosary (*tasbih*) of one thousand beads that was worn around the neck when it was not being used for invocations.

Surprisingly, state officials did not see a threat in Abu Muhammad Salih's creation of a Sufi-led pilgrimage caravan to Mecca and Medina. In organizing and maintaining this caravan, he relied on the widespread network of the followers of the Andalusian shaykh Abu Madyan (d. 1198), who supplied and protected Sufi pilgrims in regions of North Africa beyond the range of governmental authority. All aspirants to the Magiriyya were required to perform the Hajj before being initiated

---

[18] On Abu Muhammad Salih see Ibid, 138-144. The main primary source for this information was published as a critical edition and doctoral thesis by Mohamed Rais, *Aspect du Mysticisme marocain au VIIe-VIIIe/XIIIe-XIVe siècle à travers l'analyse critique de l'ouvrage al-Minhaj al-wadih fi tahqiq karamat Abu Muhammad Salih* (Université de Provence Aix-Marseille I, 1995-96).

as members. As the number of disciples grew, Abu Muhammad Salih sent the more able of them to the towns and cities of the central and eastern Maghrib, where they set up satellite centers for the shelter and provisioning of pilgrims. Sufi aspirants who did not have the money to finance their own pilgrimage were supplied with provisions by Ribat Asafi and traveled toward the east in groups, spending the night in Bedouin encampments or in hostels that had been established for this purpose. Upon arriving in Alexandria, Cairo, and the holy cities of Mecca, Medina, and Jerusalem, the pilgrims would stay at *fanadiq al-Maghariba* or *buyut al-Maghariba* (Hostels or Houses of the Westerners) that were founded by Abu Muhammad Salih's son Ahmad (d. 1262). As chief administrator of the main *Funduq al-Maghariba* in Alexandria, Ahmad appointed his own son Ibrahim, whose descendants managed the Egyptian end of the pilgrimage network for several generations.

By the time of Abu Muhammad Salih's death, the pilgrimage movement had developed to such an extent that the shaykh's successors opened it up for general membership. Ahmad al-Magiri decoupled the pilgrimage association from the Magiriyya Sufi order and created a separate organization called *al-Ta'ifa al-Hujjajiyya* (The Pilgrims' Society). To oversee this society, he appointed an independent group of administrators, whose primary function was not to train disciples, but to facilitate the flow of pilgrims to and from the holy cities. Eventually, the Magiriyya Sufi order and the Pilgrims' Society became so fully integrated into the social life of southern Morocco beyond Marrakech that Ribat Asafi became the de facto capital of this region. The Marinid rulers of the Far Maghrib confirmed this influence after their conquest of Marrakech in 1268. In that year, Sultan Abu Yusuf appointed 'Isa (d. 1299), the last surviving son of Abu Muhammad Salih, governor of Asafi and its environs.

The institutions created by Abu Muhammad Salih and his sons were certainly impressive, and perhaps unique in the history of Sufism. But did they constitute civil society? Let's look first at the liberal democratic alternative proposed by Jefferson, Tocqueville, and Dewey. When contrasted with state-based institutions, the Magiriyya Sufi order could certainly be seen as a "bottom-up" voluntary association that promoted Islamic education, ethical values, systematic training, opportunity (for males) without regard to social status, and shared notions of community. Most members of the order also shared a similar social standing, level of education, and temperament. Finally, the Magiriyya Sufi order and the Pilgrims' Society created social capital by fostering mutual trust and respect, promoted the general good over individual interests, and even created a sort of proto-national sentiment by promoting a sense of "Westernness" with the Far Maghrib as its cultural epicenter.

Where these institutions do not fit the liberal democratic model is in their failure to promote democratic self-government and the expression of minority viewpoints. Such a charge, of course, is unfair and anachronistic. Muslim societies were not liberal democracies and did not follow the tenets of political correctness. But that is precisely the point. The attempt to find precedents for liberal democracy in premodern Islam is itself an anachronistic exercise. Such exercises are often used by contemporary Muslims to avoid admitting the necessity of innovation. Anachronistically conceived "precedents" for modern institutions provide cover for Muslims who do not want to be accused of breaking tradition. It is easier to claim that modern concepts were latent in the traditions of Islam, or that "True Islam" really intended modern interpretations than to acknowledge that certain understandings of Islam have become obsolete. The reconstruction of tradition is indeed a slippery slope, but there is little advantage to denying the existence of real problems and pretending that traditions do not change.

The comparative fit is only slightly better when the Magiriyya and the Pilgrims' Society are assessed according to Rousseau's view of civil society. From the point of view of their leadership, both organizations were "top-down" institutions. They were created by a single family and depended in part on familial connections for their successful operation. In this sense, they were more like family firms than voluntary associations. However, the Magiriyya Sufi order might be said to constitute a Body Politic because it started as a free association of equals in which the participants were united toward a common goal. The Magiriyya, like all Sufi orders, was built around a sort of implied social contract, which was based on the acceptance of common doctrines and practices. John Locke would have termed this "tacit acceptance" of the social contract. One of the most important aspects of this contract for the Magiriyya was the fact that membership in the order was based on kinship with other Imazighen in the supra-tribal category known as Masmuda (pl. *Masamida*). This relation implied not only common kinship, but also a common language (Tamazight) and a common cultural-geographical orientation (highlanders versus lowlanders). The practice of basing membership in Sufi orders on supra-tribal ethnic relations is unique to the Far Maghrib and perhaps Central Asia. Common ethnic, linguistic, and religious ties are powerful reinforcements for feelings of social solidarity and notions of the Body Politic, as any Serbian or Croatian nationalist might attest.

Education and Value Formation. The final example of potential civil society formation to be discussed in this paper is that of the Sufi reformer 'Abdullah al-Habti (d. 1555), who was active in the region of Shafshawen between the city of Fez and the Rif mountains in northern Morocco.[19] Habti was a member of the Jazuliyya Sufi order, which carried out a widespread series of reforms in the fifteenth and sixteenth centuries. The Jazuliyya originated the Sufi concept of the "Muhammadan Way" (*al-Tariqa al-Muhammadiyya*), which spread as far as India and Southeast Asia through Ottoman intermediaries in Egypt and the Levant. Under the Jazuliyya, the Muhammadan Way went beyond following the external aspects of the Sunna and included the assimilation of an inspirational sense of spirituality that was linked to Ibn 'Arabi's (d. 1240) concept of the "Muhammadan Reality" (*al-haqiqa al-Muhammadiyya*).[20] Education was fundamental to the Jazuliyya program of reform because without the development of the proper consciousness, effective change was thought to be impossible.

---

[19] See Cornell, *Realm of the Saint*, 266-269. The best account of Habti's activities can be found in 'Abd al-Qadir al-'Afiya, *al-Hayat al-siyasiyya wa al-ijtima'iyya wa al-fikriyya bi-Shafshawan wa ahwaziha khilal al-qarn al-'ashir al-hijri* (Rabat, 1982).

[20] Cornell, *Realm of the Saint*, 196-229.

Habti was the most systematic reformer of all the Sufis discussed in this paper. Also, the purposefulness of his program and his attention to education and value formation make his project uniquely comparable to pragmatic and liberal democratic notions of civil society. Habti's reform project brought together Sufism, jurisprudence, and dogma, and depended on a thorough knowledge of local cultures. He planned his project with his friend and former classmate Abu al-Qasim ibn Khajju ("Son of Khadija," d. 1550) who was a judge for the Banu Hassan clan of Sharifs (descendants of the Prophet Muhammad through the line of al-Hasan ibn 'Ali). Habti and Ibn Khajju sat down and mapped out a program of social and religious reform for Shafshawen and its surrounding region as one would map out a political campaign today. The third member of their team was Habti's wife Aminah, Ibn Khajju's sister, who was a fully trained legist in her own right. Aminah bint Khajju presided over a Sufi *zawiyya* next to that of her husband, where she taught the same curriculum to the women of Shafshawen that her husband taught to the men.

Habti's critiques of local society and suggestions for reform are preserved in a remarkable poem entitled *al-Alfiyya as-saniyya fi tanbih al-'amma wa al-khassa 'ala ma awqa'a min at-taghyir fi al-milla al-Islamiyya* (The Exalted Thousand Verses Awakening the Masses and the Elites to the Deviations that have Occurred in the Islamic Community).[21] The thousand-verse (*alfiyya*) format employed in this work had long been used in the Far Maghrib as a method for teaching grammar. In Habti's hands, it became a tool of social commentary and political propaganda that recalled the pamphlets and leaflets then being printed by Protestant activists in Europe. This purpose was facilitated by the repetitive nature of the genre's *rajaz* rhyme-pattern, which eased memorization and smoothed the process of dissemination in a society that had yet to adopt the printing press.

Habti believed that the cause of the social ills besetting his country was a general loss of faith. This was exacerbated by ignorance and illiteracy, frequent contact with Portuguese soldiers and merchants,

---

[21] 'Abdallah ibn Muhammad al-Habti, *al-Alfiyya as-saniyya* (Rabat, Bibliothèque Hassania ms. 2808)

and excessive loyalty to tradition (*taqlid* or *'ada*). In particular, Habti castigates the religious and political elites of Shafshawen for their lack of concern about the moral decay surrounding them. The worst offenders are the official scholars and jurists. Habti calls some of them "rabbis" (*ahbar*) because of their concern for the letter of the law instead of its spirit. Others he calls "priests" (*rahban*), because their main concern is their sense of entitlement to government sinecures.

Habti was a strong advocate of the education of women. He was concerned that mothers were unprepared to instill an adequate understanding of Islam in their offspring. However, rather than blaming women for their ignorance, he instead focused on their husbands and fathers, accusing them of shirking their responsibilities. According to Habti, each married man is responsible for the moral and intellectual upbringing of his family. The family is an Islamic community in miniature, and the father is the Imam of his community. Uneducated family members are burdens on the community. Ignorant mothers produce ignorant children, and ignorant children become sinful adults. The sinfulness of adults undermines the moral basis of society, and the circle of ignorance begins again. To ensure that mothers were properly equipped to teach their children moral values, some of Habti's disciples even went so far as to make brides pass exams in Islamic dogma before witnessing their marriage contracts.[22]

Habti's educational program for both men and women emphasized instruction in the Shari'a and a reading knowledge of the Arabic language. As an initial step, he and Ibn Khajju would go to a village or tribal encampment and convince its leaders of the need for change. Later, they would assemble the inhabitants of the village and quiz them on what they knew about the teachings of Islam. Subjects that were stressed in these question-and-answer sessions included Islamic history, the concept of monotheism, the Five Pillars of Islam, bodily hygiene and purification, and rules pertaining to the monthly periods of women and the waiting period (*'idda*) after a divorce or the death of a husband. Habti and Ibn Khajju would remain in a locality until its leaders or

---

[22] See Musa ibn 'Ali al-Wazzani, *Risala fi ta'lim al-'aqida* (Madrid, Biblioteca Nacional ms. 5168)

elders signed a formal contract, swearing that they would forbid usury, encourage daily prayers, and follow the Sunna. If a mosque did not exist in the village, Habti would supervise its construction. If alcohol were sold, he would convince its purveyors to leave or go into another line of business.

Although Habti focused most of his attention on social and educational reform, he did not overlook the jihad against the Portuguese, who controlled much of Morocco in the first half of the sixteenth century. He and Ibn Khajju traveled widely, calling for Muslim unity in the face of the Iberian threat. They also sent letters to rulers, jurists, students of the law, and official notaries encouraging them to support jihad for the preservation of Islam. Habti was especially concerned that the authorities resist the conversion of Muslims to Christianity, which had begun to occur in the border areas near the Portuguese enclaves of Tangier and Alcazar. He was also concerned about the large Andalusian refugee populations in the cities of Shafshawen and Tetuan. While they provided welcome reinforcements for jihad, they also introduced European customs that undermined traditional Islamic values.

The example of Habti, the social reformer and jihadist, brings the present discussion back to the Al Qaeda figures mentioned at the beginning of this paper. However, the similarity between such modern Muslim extremists and an early modern reformer such as Habti is only superficial. Although Habti was a traditionalist, his criticism of blind or unthinking tradition would make him a "critical traditionalist" by today's standards. For example, his view of the common good included women as moral and intellectual actors, something that Al Qaeda and their Taliban supporters would never accept. Habti also chose to negotiate, rather than impose his reforms. Signing contracts with tribal leaders and village elders not only committed these leaders to his reform project, it also demonstrated Habti's respect for self-government. By respecting local authority structures, he distanced himself from the state and showed that he could be an honest broker. More indirectly, he tacitly acknowledged self-government through decentralization and highlighted the importance of consensus to the process of social change.

In all of his activities Habti displayed a temperament that was consistently consensual, following well-known precepts about the value of consultation (*Shura*) as a means of determining the general will. For this reason, we might possibly call Habti, without too much anachronism, a proto-democrat. Equally importantly, he was a strong supporter of the notion, shared by Jefferson and the democratic pragmatists, of enlightenment through education. Like Dewey, who was concerned about the dangers of an uninformed electorate, Habti was aware that ignorant parents raised ignorant children, and that ignorant children grow up to be ignorant adults who are incapable of acting in their best interests. Rather than defining their interests for them, as totalitarians tend to do, Habti gave people the intellectual and philosophical tools to make their own decisions. Key to this strategy was his view that the Sunna was not just a set of behaviors by which unthinking tradition could be perpetuated, but rather that it was a mode of consciousness which, when instilled in the believer, guided one like a beacon toward the best action. Habti's project depended at all stages on the accumulation and expenditure of social capital. In this respect, he was a sort of "Jeffersonian democrat" before Jefferson. Might it not be better, however, to let Habti interrogate the present and say that Jefferson was an American version of a "Jazulite Populist?"

CREATIVE IMPROVISATION

At the beginning of this paper it was noted that a post-liberal approach to democracy and civil society in Islam depended on a combination of textual reasoning through scripture and a critical and historical analysis of religious and social institutions as they were manifested in the real world of Islamic practice. It was also proposed that effective arguments for democracy in the Muslim world must be based on a thorough understanding of traditional Islamic models of government as well as the comparative study of moral and political philosophy in Islam and the West, including the varieties of democratic alternatives that have appeared in Europe, America, and elsewhere. The foregoing discussion should have established beyond any doubt that the idea of civil society, like democracy itself, is a contested concept, and that traditional Islamic institutions can only approximate the notion of civil society at best. Bearing these points in mind, the following conclusions may be proposed:

1. Civil society is a Western concept. It is dependent on democracy, which is also a Western concept. There is no "Islamic" democracy or "Islamic" civil society per se. The idea of civil society came out of discussions in Enlightenment and post-Enlightenment political philosophy about the building blocks of democracy and the locus of self-rule. It is doubtful whether this concept, as originally formulated, exists anywhere in premodern Islamic discourse. Premodern voluntary institutions in Sufism only approximated the notion of civil society to a greater or lesser degree. In none of cases discussed above, including Habti's, did the Islamic example meet the liberal-democratic criterion of fostering democratic self-rule.

2. There is no need to Islamize civil society. The idea that a concept has to have its intellectual and epistemological roots in a primary Islamic text is a fundamentalist notion that flies in the face of Islamic intellectual history. It is more a strategy of power than an interpretive statement. Classical Islamic political theory had as much to do with Persian notions of kingship as it did with the Qur'an and the Sunna. In legal terms, democracy and civil society can be incorporated into Islamic social life as 'urfi (customary) concepts. This was a widely accepted practice in the *fiqh* tradition and it enabled the spread of Islam into many areas, such as Minangkabau in West Sumatra, where local traditions had little in common with the Middle Eastern cultural milieu out of which Islam originally developed. Civil society and democracy can be incorporated as aspects of Islamic practice through either the Maliki concept

of *maslaha* (public interest) or the Hanafi concepts of istihsan and *bid'a hasana* (public interest and positive innovation).

3. We should avoid buying into the modernist notion that the task of an enlightened society is "not to conserve and transmit the whole of its existing achievements, but only such as make for a better future society."[23] The problem with this statement is that it serves two preconceived agendas. On the one hand it serves the fundamentalist agenda by justifying the elimination of the majority of religious history as "dead wood from the past," and the reconstruction of religion on instrumentalist grounds. This has been the strategy of Islamic modernist reform since the end of the nineteenth century. The second problem with this statement is that it justifies the modernist agenda of freeing the present from the past, by assuming, as Gandhi did, that "the past could be treated as though it were a pool of resources, a standing reserve, on which the subject of political modernity could draw as needed."[24]

4. Muslims must develop a post-colonial, post-fundamentalist, and post-modernist (not post-modern, but post-liberal-modernity) view of the past that allows the past and present of Islam to enter into a dialogic relationship with each other. Muslims need to rediscover the intellectual and cultural traditions of Islam, not to reproduce them as romanticized simulacra, but rather to guide religious, moral, and social thinking toward a new critique of the present. I call this stance "critical traditionalism." Dipesh Chakrabarty uses another term, "decisionism," which he opposes to modernist historicism. By decisionism, Chakrabarty means a simultaneous orientation toward the present and the past that "allows the critic to talk about the present and the past as though there were concrete, value-laden choices to be made with regard to both . . . The critic is guided by his or her values to choose the most desirable,

---

[23] Ambedkar quoted in Ibid, 246.

[24] Ibid.

sane, and wise future for humanity."[25] Chakrabarty believes that this model differs from the "storage-attic" approach to tradition advocated by Gandhi, in that it "represents a freedom from history as well as a freedom to respect the aspects of 'tradition' considered useful to building the desired future."[26] For me, this statement is still too historicist. Instead, I prefer Ashis Nandy's attempt to restore a dialogical conversation between the past and the present, interspersed, in the Islamic case, by "principled forgetfulness and silence," as regards, for example, the subject of slavery, the oppression of women, and religious bigotry. Constructions of the past, says Nandy, "are primarily responsible to the present and to the future; they are meant neither for the archivist nor for the archaeologist. They try to expand human options by reconfiguring the past and transcending it through *creative improvisations* . . . The past shapes the present and future but the present and the future also shape the past. Some scholars . . . are . . . willing to redefine, perhaps even transfigure, the past to open up the future. The choice is not cognitive, but moral and political, in the best sense of the term."[27]

---

[25] Ibid, 247

[26] Ibid.

[27] Ibid, 247-248.

Social Reform
in Muslim Society Today

by
Professor Yusuf Da Costa, Ph.D.

Social Reform
in Muslim Society Today

by Yusuf da Costa, Ph.D.

أعوذ بالله من الشيطان الرجيم

بسم الله الرحمن الرحيم الحمد لله بـــر العالمين و الصلاة و السلام

على أشرف المرسلين سيد محمد و على اله و أصحابه أجمعين

لا حول و لا قوة إلا بالله العلي العظيم

INTRODUCTION

*T*his paper focuses primarily on those internal factors within Muslim society (or the Ummah, as that society is generally called) that have brought about the present state of fracturing of that society, and what can be recommended to commence a process of reform within that society. Of course, there are many external factors that might also have had either negative or positive impacts on that society but those factors are for another discussion.

If one speaks about reform, one must know exactly and as truthfully as possible what one is faced with. It is, therefore, necessary, at the outset, to examine whether the term Ummah as originally used is in fact still applicable to the Muslim population of the world today. The word is generally translated as "Muslim society". "Community of believers" or "Nation of Muhammad (s.a.w.s.)", and is considered as the major form of spatial organization applicable to the followers of the religion of Islam. This spatial organization, by its very nature, transcends national boundaries and any other social and political divides between people. In terms of this understanding, Braibanti (1985, p. 1)[1] refers to the Ummah as "the territorially dispersed but

---

[1] Braibanti, R. 1985. *Toward the realization of ummah: the televance of the Philippine dar al-harb*. The American Journal of Islamic Social Sciences, vol. 2, no. 1, 1985, pp. 1-14.

spiritually unified global Islamic commonwealth". In providing another aspect of the meaning of the term, Irving et al (1979, p. 29)2 state that "the Muslim ummah, community of faith, represents a people committed to this Book (i.e. the Qur'an) – those who believe in it, stand by it and derive their identity from it." Braibanti (1985, pp. 3-4) sees this spatial structure as one of considerable sophistication and although it is perenially disrupted by "intra-Islamic rivalries" and "non-Islamic forces", there is "ample evidence to suggest that the structure is gaining in strength." Today the Muslim community comprises more than one billion people or over 20% of the world's population.

The Ummah was never meant to be a loose spatial structure held together by some mysterious forces. We know that this is not true. We know that there is no such binding "spiritual" factor, and we also know that there is no such "universal commitment to the Qur'an." Let us see what the Qur'an says:

إِنَّمَا الْمُؤْمِنُونَ إِخْوَةٌ

The believers are but a single brotherhood (xlix: 10).

The following Prophetic Tradition explains this:

On the authority of Abu Hurayra (r.a.), who said: The Messenger of Allah (s.a.w.s.) said: Do not envy one another; do not inflate prices one to another; do not turn away from one another; and do not undercut one another, *but be you, O servants of Allah, brothers. A Muslim is the brother of a Muslim: he neither oppresses him nor does he fail him*, he neither lies to him nor does he hold him in contempt. Piety is right here – and he pointed to his breast three times. It is evil enough for a man to hold his brother Muslim in contempt. *The whole of a Muslim for another Muslim is inviolable: his blood, his property, and his honour* (Muslim).

---

2 Irving, T.B., Ahmad, K. & Ahsan, M.M. 1979. *The Qur'an: basic teachings.* London: The Islamic Foundation.

The above verse and Prophetic Tradition entrench mutual respect, help and honour for each other amongst the believers. It is a "linking of hearts" of those who are classified by the Qur'an as believers not only because of a set of common beliefs and practices but also because of what they mean to each other with regard to mutual security and protection, common action and a common sharing of resources. This was how the Ummah was that was established by the Prophet (s.a.w.s.). Let us measure the state of this population with regard to only two matters:

(a) "A Muslim does not fail another Muslim": There is no doubt that large sections of the world's Muslim population have been deserted by the rest of the world's Muslim population. We continue happily with our lives while there are millions of Muslims experiencing the most indescribable suffering. We in fact "leave them to their own fate". In the same way we left Muslims under the Communist regimes to "their own fate" while mosques and madrassahs were closed, mosques converted to shopping malls, scholars killed and persecuted, and the public practice of Islam banned (I had personally seen how Islam had been ravaged in Uzbekistan, previously part of the U.S.S.R.). At another level, we find thousands of Muslims who fled their own countries to find refuge and safety in the countries of the West. Muslims have to admit that not a single Muslim country is prepared to give help, or is capable of giving help, when any section of the world's Muslim population needs support to solve, for example, the massive poverty as in Africa. It appears that mutual support and protection, an essential part of how the world's Muslim community is supposed to operate, has largely disappeared.

(b) "The whole of a Muslim for another Muslim is inviolable." Let us take "his blood", as an example. The history of Islam is littered with countless examples of the killing of Muslims by Muslims, and this has continued up to today. Surely, this must have had, and is most probably still having, a massively eroding effect on any of the social cement that might have been keeping Muslims together is a single spatial structure. And it must also be having a major detrimental impact on the religious integrity of those who have been decision makers in these killings. And possibly the killing of Sayyidatuna Uthman (r.a.) started the process of fracturing of the Ummah established by the Messenger (s.a.w.s.). Perhaps his killing was the first nail in the coffin, and all the other killings, especially of those so closely related to the Prophet (s.a.w.s.), must have added many of the original nails.

Let us at this stage consider another aspect of the deliberate and consistent disobedience of the rules of Islam by Muslims. An important rule in Islam is that children, women and old people should not be deliberately killed, neither those people with whom a covenant had been made. The latter refers to those non-Muslims living under the protection of a Muslim government. There are countless examples of how these rules have been ignored in the "cause of Islam", and the largely almost unbelievable silence of the world's Muslim community on these matters.

If one considers all these factors and events mentioned, one has to ask: Can one describe the present state of the world's Muslim population as one in which the population can be said to be organized in a spatial structure bound by a common socio-religious cement of beliefs and practices? My answer to this is no. Other than the above factors and events, which have been steadily eroding away the adhesive that originally kept the Ummah together, there are also a number of other divisive forces, which have contributed to this disintegration. Movements for independence during the 20th century gave rise to highly independent states which are prepared to go to war with each other as the need arises, to suppress the voice of Islam when it challenges the Islamic legitimacy of the state, and for different factions within a country to go to war with each other in competition for hegemony. Other divides, which have played havoc with "the brotherhood of believers" are the Sunni-Shia one (which sometimes degenerates into open conflict, as in Pakistan), racial divides (genocide against the Kurds in Iraq and racial divisions within Muslim minorities as in South Africa, for example), divides based on aqidah (the Deobandi- Berelvi differences which appear to have originated in the Indian sub-continent but is now found all over the world in different forms), and political divides as a product of the relations between nations. These are other than the many factors, too many to mention, that divide people into different and opposing groups within Muslim countries and within Muslim minorities in non-Muslim countries.

Add to all this the massive poverty, and all that goes with that, in parts of the Muslim world especially in Africa, the genocide against Muslims in Bosnia, the dehumanization of women, the adoption of ways of life that are destroying the Islamic fabric of many countries, the regular killing of large sections of Muslim populations in Africa, and major disobedience of the Shari'ah almost on national scales, then one can understand why there is very little left of the Ummah as a reality today. This disobedience involves especially the disregard for the teachings in the Qur'an by processes of "erasure". In many parts of the world large sections of the Qur'an have been "erased" as Muslims adopt other ways of life and discourses. To this may be added the major neglect of the Prophetic Practice that I have seen in different Muslim countries.

OUR STAND

Despite all these negative factors, there are still large groups of Muslims throughout the world whose attachment to Islam takes priority in their lives, and it is these Muslims that have to become the vanguard of social reform wherever they live. However:

(a) We, first of all, have to face up to the truth of the real state of this community, of both its past and present history. In order to do this, we need to change the "eye glasses" through which we normally look at the world, and to pose the questions about Islam and its adherents in another way. It is not possible to be objective and honest about our state of affairs if we adopt simplistic approaches to the socio-religious behavior of the Muslims since the time of the Prophet (s.a.w.s.), and refuse to remove the intellectual cataracts that blur our understanding of that history.

Perhaps because I am a Muslim, the shame is greatest because we so comfortably say and believe that we function in terms of the Truth when in fact throughout the world "Muslims" have become of the greatest distorters of the Divine teachings despite all their suffering and humiliation over the centuries. They do not need their enemies to distort their religion. They have become masters in cutting their religious cloth to suit their politics. And this applies especially to those groups who profess to be acting in the Cause of God.

There is very little left of Islam with regard to what many of us do although we glibly mention the Name of God to justify the acts barbarism that is sweeping different parts of the world in the name of religion. We say that people are fighting a war against Islam and we do not mention the war against Islam being waged in "Muslim" countries. Why are we so dishonest? Where is this Islam that is being fought against? In what country? People need not fight Islam. The Muslims have destroyed a large part of Islam themselves. People need only pick up the pieces if they so wish. Do you know that it is one of the ironies of history that there is more freedom of religion in the West than in some "Muslim" countries. South Africa is filled with refugees that have gone there to practice Islam freely and make a living. Large numbers of these refugees are from "Muslim" countries.

(b) We must try very hard to utilize our physical and mental resources for this process of obedience, and draw whosoever we can to become part of this process. Only in our obedience to Him, can we bring about those social changes that are needed to enhance that obedience. Whatever happens in the world, whatever the socio-political struggles, if they are not being conducted to enhance that obedience, then they are not being conducted in His Name. This does not mean that one should not help others to ease the burdens of people but one should be aware when such relief of burdens is in His Name or not, and one should then work hard to change the complexion of such relief so that it is done in His Name. Allah Almighty instructs us in the Qur'an: K´n´ ansar Allah Be helpers (in the Cause) of Allah. The Qur'an provides the final word on all matters.

(c) Perhaps the major weakness of the world's Muslim population is the non-existence of a central authority to which all the Muslims submit. The large arrangement of divides, the geographical spread of this population, the deculturation of large sections of the population, the spread of secularism and sectarianism and the large number of different and opposing authorities, nationally and internationally, each one claiming to be the voice of the Muslims, make the establishment of such an authority almost impossible under the present circumstances. Without such a central authority, there is no way that the Muslims can adopt at least some kind of uniform response to situations that face all or some of them.

(d) We need to consider a major redefinition of terms in reaction to the realities facing us, based on the fact that we are busy with the human response to a revealed religion. The word Islam is one such term. Islam is a Divine Message, and we are busy investigating how this message has come to operate amongst its recipients, and how the recipients have internalized the message and responded to it. Whatever the socio-political arrangements we have come to in our lives, whatever the nature of the problems facing us, whatever the manner we consider our Divine service to be, in the final analyses, Islam must be seen as a means of obtaining Divine Satisfaction. In a sense, we have to clear the table, and place the standards and values set by this revealed religion as the only standards and values in terms of which the affairs in the Muslim community have to operate. And these standards and values, clearly spelt out and defined according to the Divine Message, must be used to re-program the minds of our young people. There is just no way that we can win the "battles of the minds" by creating a bulwark against deculturation if we are unclear as to what we wish to do and wish to achieve.

(e) Perhaps we have to start thinking of looking at Islam through spiritual and not non-spiritual lenses. Islam began with an immense incursion of spirituality into the affairs of humanity when the first revelation came. And all the other human affairs initiated by Islam came as a consequence of that incursion, and all these affairs were constantly fed by further such incursions. The spiritual dimension of Islam sustained all the socio-economic structures that developed under the religion. All the time it was God talking, and what He was saying and what His Messenger (s.a.w.s.) was saying were implemented in the lives of the Muslims at the time. Over the centuries, the geographical spread of Islam brought it into contact with other cultures and socio-economic structures, and these cultures and socio-economic structures together with the many factors mentioned in this paper, impinged on the religion. There is just no way those two cultures can meet in the same spatial context, and mutual diffusion does not take place. Of course, in the process, God and His Messenger were being heard less and less. We see this every day in the communities in which we live.

(f) I want to seriously suggest that we have to devise ways and means of drawing on the immense intellectual and spiritual reservoirs in this religion for both individual and social sustenance. Islam has been hijacked by ways of thinking that do not give enough regard to the religion's spiritual dimension, and we are being short-changed in the process. Islam was never meant to be only for the "minds" of human beings. It was meant primarily for their "hearts". And the failure of Muslims to come to terms with the world, and to deal properly with their problems, is because God and His Messenger (s.a.w.s.) have been taken out of their position of centrality in our lives. As religious beings, we have to look to our religion as to how we are going to handle social reform within Muslim societies.

WHAT SHOULD WE TRY TO DO?

Before considering the "big" things we can suggest to be done, I want to describe the South African experience with regard to work at the very grassroots level.

THE SOUTH AFRICAN EXPERIENCE

In 1998, our community decided to tackle some of our community's social ills by re-introducing tasawwuf [known in the West as Sufism] and spirituality.

The growth of this group has been phenomenal. About 600 persons attended the first public congregational dhikr or chanting ceremony in the country at a mosque in July 1999. At present (December, 2004) over four hundred persons have taken bay'ah [initiation] but we have large numbers of especially relatively poor supporters. By now, the group has become the largest and most active group, at least in the Cape, which is attached to an official mainstream tariqah line. Although it had originally bought a building for a zawiyyah, the building has been sold because we work in mosques and other community structures, in order to work amongst the poor. We have no more need for a zawiyyah as such because we go where the people are, especially the poor people. The way we work in Cape Town has now been extended to Port Elizabeth and Durban.

The following are some of the group's activities:

(a) It has six congregational dhikrs every weekend. These include a big general congregational dhikr in a mosque somewhere in the Cape Peninsula on a Friday evening, two ladies' dhikrs on a Saturday afternoon, a congregational dhikr at some mosque in the adjacent country area on a Saturday evening, and a congregational dhikr in one of the Indigenous African areas on a Sunday morning. The dhikrs are followed by talks on Mainstream Islam, or a reading of one of the lectures of sufi Shaykhs.

(b) Bringing people into Islam from the indigenous African areas, and organizing classes in those areas: Ladies from the organization go out every Sunday morning to teach in these areas. For this purpose also, the organization has appointed a full-time Islamic missionary for these areas. We also provide food, clothing and medical care where needed.

(c) Upgrading religious structures in the Indigenous African areas: The pathetic condition of these structures forced the organization to start this work. An attempt to get the larger Muslim community assistance to help in the upgrading failed hopelessly.

(d) Every Friday evening murids from the Indigenous African areas are brought by taxi to wherever the congregational dhikrs are being held, and for the first time lectures on Islam are being heard and reversions to Islam are being done in Xhosa in some of these mosques.

(e) In August 2003 our community took a major organizational step with the launching of An-Nisa', a women's only group with the specific task of working amongst women.i This task involves the empowerment of women through education and spirituality. Under the leadership of a committee of ladies, the group has started on a series of workshops to perform the specific tasks allocated to them. Three of the workshops that impacted well on the community were those on Muslim Personal Law, Cancer and Abortion. Through these workshops and programs on radio, the organization is slowly spreading its message to the community.

THE BIGGER THINGS WE SHOULD WORK TOWARDS

Active steps should flow from our deliberations for the use of literature and all possible forms of mass media to spread the message of Mainstream Islam as the only true Islam, and to counteract, at all possible levels, the hijacking of Islam by deviant groups. Structures should be set up in all countries with this as its primary task. If it is working in South Africa, it can work elsewhere. We should get-out of the confines of our own institutions and "get our hands dirty" with work in the Cause of Allah Almighty. And an essential part of our work should be to start closing the divides operating in Muslim communities.

When it comes to major social reform involving large communities and societies, there is no way that such reform can be launched for Muslims only because of the population and religious mix of such societies and communities. Muslims have to work towards social improvements for all peoples wherever such improvements are needed.

(i) Conference should call on national and international agencies (or link up with them) to organize assistance for major programs of social reform wherever they are needed. Large parts of Africa, for example, need infrastructures, health care, housing, and education. Such programs should strike a proper balance in agriculture between subsistence and commercial farming, and should utilize industrial and technological growth for the benefit of the nations concerned. Large parts of the population of Africa and other parts of the world are living below the subsistence level. People need work, food, water and clothing. According to a report of the International Labour Organization, about 1,4 billion people in the world earn less than 2 dollars a day, and of these about 40% earn less than one dollar a day. About 200 million people are unemployed (Cape Argus, 07:12:04, p. 4).

(ii) Special programs should be organized to save the world's natural environments, and for the intelligent use of the world's natural resources for the benefit of its peoples. In many countries, such as the Indian sub-continent, the destruction of the natural environment for commercial farming has brought about large-scale starvation because of the depletion of the biomass. Conference should take a stand on this.

(iii) Parts of the world are being ravaged by HIV/Aids. South Africa with 2% of the world's population has 72% of the world HIV/Aids victims. Add to this the massive abortion rates throughout the world (in the USA alone there are 1,3 million abortions every year), then one realizes the immensity of the task facing us with regard to sexual practice in the world. A very strong religious message should go out to the world on the need to go back to the teachings of the Divine Law on sexual practice and abortions, and possibly the Ugandan experience of bringing down the HIV/Aids rates should be studied, and used as an example of how to deal with this scourge. Muslims should participate actively in tackling this problem, and not say it is not our concern.

There must be in all of us the determination to become "activists" in the Cause of God. We cannot allow the present decline of the world's values to go unchallenged. Muslims need to be in the forefront of transformation.

And we appeal for Divine support in all that we do, and that what we do should be for His sake. And Allah knows best.

Principles of Leadership
in War & Peace

by
Shaykh Muhammad Hisham Kabbani

Chairman, Islamic Supreme Council of America

Principles of Leadership
in War & Peace

by Shaykh Muhammad Hisham Kabbani

*I*n this presentation, we would like to shed light on the meaning of Jihād, a term that has become universally known today. One can find countless interpretations of this term which differ from its true spirit and the meaning that God intended in the Holy Qur'ān and in the narrations of the Prophet ﷺ. Instead of adhering to these canonical principles, people today are use the term Jihād in a way that suits their own whims without realizing the damage they are causing to Islam and Muslims.

What is meant by Jihād? It certainly does not mean "holy war." That is *"al-Harb al-muqaddasah"* in Arabic. Indeed, nowhere in the Qur'ān can one find any term that expresses the meaning "holy war." Rather, the meaning of combative Jihād expressed in the Qur'ān or Hadith is simply war.

That said, we will show in this presentation that Jihād, in the classical sense, also means much more than that. In fact, Jihād is a comprehensive term which traditionally has been defined as being composed of fourteen different aspects, only one of which involves warfare.

In this presentation we will explain unambiguously the different aspects of Jihād defined by the Prophet ﷺ together with what renowned mainstream Muslims scholars have written about this subject, citing them at length in order to arrive at an accurate understanding of this term.

Islamic thought includes all scholarly opinions rendered in amplification of Islam's core principles, its simplicity and its tender and compassionate approach to all aspects of human relations.

Today, there are many individuals who study Islam from a superficial point of view and emerge with their own ideas and novel interpretations which often diverge greatly from established legal opinions. Such studies lack any real basis in Islamic jurisprudence. However, this fact is not apparent to most non-Muslims, and these misguided proclamations give them a distorted understanding of Islam.

In this presentation, we will return to the original source texts that discuss the issue of Jihād in order to explain its various facets and clarify its meaning once and for all.

THE MEANING OF JIHĀD

The general meaning of Jihād is "to struggle." Jihād derives from the word juhd, which means "to struggle." The meaning of Jihād fī sabīlillāh, Struggle in the Way of God, is striving to exhaust the self in seeking the Divine Presence and promoting God's Word, which He made the Way to Paradise. For that reason God said:

$$\text{جَاهِدُوا فِي اللهِ حَقَّ جِهَادِهِ}$$

And strive hard (jāhidū) in (the way of) God, (such) a striving a is due to Him; [22:78]

It is essential to understand that under the term jāhidū come many different categories of Jihād. The common understanding of Jihād as referring only to war is refuted by this tradition of the Prophet's ﷺ:

حدثنا عبد الرحمن بن مهدي عن سفيان عن علقمة بن مرثد عن طارق بن شهاب أن

رجلا سأل رسول الله صلى الله عليه وسلم وقد وضع رجله في الغرز أي الجهاد أفضل قال

كلمة حق عند سلطان جائر

A man asked the Prophet ﷺ "Which Jihād is best?" The Prophet ﷺ said, "The most excellent Jihād is to say the word of truth in front of a tyrant."[1]

The fact that the Prophet ﷺ mentioned this Jihād as "most excellent" demonstrates that there are many different forms of Jihād.

IBN QAYYIMS' FOURTEEN CATEGORIES OF JIHĀD

Islamic scholars, from the time of the Prophet ﷺ until today, have categorized Jihād into at least fourteen distinct categories. A cogent discussion of these categories is found in the book Zād al-Ma'ād, by Ibn Qayyim al-Jawzīyyah. According to him, the categories of Jihād are:

1. JIHĀD AGAINST THE HYPOCRITES

1.1. By heart

1.2. By tongue

1.3. By wealth

1.4. By person.

2. JIHĀD AGAINST THE UNBELIEVERS

2.1. By heart

2.2. By tongue

2.3. By wealth

2.4. By person.

---

[1] *Musnad* of Ahmad. Similar ahadith are narrated in Abū Dawūd and Tirmidhī.

3. JIHĀD AGAINST THE DEVIL

3.1. Fighting him defensively by rejecting the false desires and slanderous doubts that he throws towards the servant.

3.2. Fighting him defensively by rejecting what he throws towards the servant of corrupt passion and desire.

4. JIHĀD OF THE SELF

4.1. Striving to seek guidance and learn the religion of truth, without which there is no felicity or happiness in life or in the hereafter.

4.2. Striving to act upon it after he has learned it, for the abstract quality of knowledge without action, even if it yields no wrong, is without benefit.

4.3. Striving to call to God and to teach the religion to someone who does not know it.

4.4. Striving with patience in seeking to call to God and bearing with patience whatever adversity comes from that for the sake of God.[2]

IBN RUSHD'S CATEGORIZATION OF JIHĀD

Ibn Rushd, in his *Muqaddimah*, divides Jihād into four categories:

1. Jihād of the heart
2. Jihād of the tongue
3. Jihād of the hand
4. Jihād of the sword.[3]

---

[2] Ibn Qayyim al-Jawzīyyah, *Zād al-Maʿād*.

[3] Ibn Rushd (known in the Western world as Averroes), *Muqaddimah*, p. 259.

JIHĀD OF THE HEART – STRUGGLE AGAINST THE SELF

The Jihād of the heart is the struggle of the individual with his or her own desires, whims, erroneous ideas and false understandings. This includes the struggle to purify the heart, to rectify one's actions and to observe the rights and responsibilities of all other human beings.

JIHĀD OF THE TONGUE – EDUCATION AND COUNSEL

Ibn Rushd defines Jihād of the tongue as:

To commend good conduct and forbid the wrong, like the type of Jihād God ordered us to fulfill against the hypocrites in His Words, *"O Prophet! Strive hard against the unbelievers and the hypocrites"* [9:73].

This is the Jihād the Prophet ﷺ waged in struggling to teach his people. It means speaking about one's cause and one's religion.

God first revealed:

$$ اقْرَأْ بِاسْمِ رَبِّكَ $$

Read *in the name of Thy Lord!* [96:1]

Thus, the first aspect of the Jihād of Education and Counsel is reading. Reading originates with the tongue.

$$ يَا أَيُّهَا النَّبِيُّ جَاهِدِ الْكُفَّارَ وَالْمُنَافِقِينَ وَاغْلُظْ عَلَيْهِمْ $$

O Prophet! strive hard [jāhid] against the unbelievers and the Hypocrites, and be firm against them. [9:73]

97

JIHĀD OF THE HAND – DEVELOPMENT OF CIVIL SOCIETY AND MATERIAL PROGRESS

Jihād of the hand includes the struggle to build the nation through material development and progress, including building up civil society, acquiring and improving every aspect of technology and societal progress in general. This includes scientific discovery, development of medical clinics and hospitals, communication, transportation, and all necessary underlying infrastructures for societal progress and advancement, including educational institutions. Building also means to open opportunities to the poor through economic programs and self-empowerment.

Another aspect of Jihād by Hand is writing, for God said:

$$ الَّذِي عَلَّمَ بِالْقَلَمِ عَلَّمَ الْإِنْسَانَ مَا لَمْ يَعْلَمْ $$

He taught by means of the pen, taught mankind what he did not know. [96:4,5]

The meaning writing includes the use of computers and all other forms of publication.

JIHĀD OF THE SWORD – COMBATIVE WAR

Finally, Jihād of the hand includes struggle by the sword (Jihādun bissayf), as when one fights the aggressor who attacks in combative war.

JIHĀD IN HISTORY AND LAW

Let us now consider the nature of Jihād more fully as it appears in the history and law of Islam. Sa'īd Ramadān Būtī, a contemporary orthodox scholar from Syria states in his seminal work Jihād in Islam[4]:

---

[4] Muhammad Sa'īd R. Al-Būtī, Jihad fīl-islām, Dar al-Fikr, Beirut, 1995.

The Prophet ﷺ invited the unbelievers peacefully, lodged protests against their beliefs and strove to remove their misgivings about Islam. When they refused any other solution, but rather declared a war against him and his message and initiated the fight, there was no alternative except to fight back.[5]

The most fundamental form of Jihād, usually overlooked in today's pursuit of newsworthy headlines, is that of presenting the message of Islam—da'wah. Thirteen years of the Prophet's ﷺ 23-year mission consisted purely of this type of Jihād. Contrary to popular belief, the word Jihād and related forms of its root word *jāhada* are mentioned in many Makkan verses in a purely non-combative context.

Combative Jihād, in the technical usage of Islamic law, means "the declaration of war against belligerent aggressors." The decision to wage combative Jihād can only be made by the leader of the nation; it is not a haphazard decision anyone may make. Moreover, the principles of Islamic jurisprudence state that the actions of the leader must be guided by the interests of the people.

THE JIHĀD OF EDUCATION

We can see that the building blocks of democracy were present in the Prophet's ﷺ message from its very outset. Through the Jihād of Education, he championed freedom of expression and debate after the chiefs of the Makkan tribes sought to suppress them during the Messenger's first years of preaching. God states in the Qur'ān:

$$ ادْعُ إِلَى سَبِيلِ رَبِّكَ بِالْحِكْمَةِ وَالْمَوْعِظَةِ الْحَسَنَةِ وَجَادِلْهُم بِالَّتِي هِيَ أَحْسَنُ إِنَّ رَبَّكَ هُوَ أَعْلَمُ بِمَن ضَلَّ عَن سَبِيلِهِ وَهُوَ أَعْلَمُ بِالْمُهْتَدِينَ $$

Invite (all) to the Way of thy Lord with wisdom and beautiful preaching; and argue with them in ways that are best and most

---

[5] Ibid., p. 44.

gracious: for thy Lord knoweth best, who have strayed from His Path, and who receive guidance. [16:125]

Thus, calling people to Islam and making them acquainted with it in all its aspects through dialogue and rhetorical persuasion is the first type of Jihād in Islam. This is referred to in the Qur'ān where God says:

فَلَا تُطِعِ الْكَافِرِينَ وَجَاهِدْهُم بِهِ جِهَادًا كَبِيرًا

So obey not the disbelievers, but strive against them (by preaching) with the utmost endeavor with it (the Qur'ān). [25:52].

Here the word "strive," *jāhidū*, is used to mean struggle by means of the tongue—preaching and exhortation—and to persevere despite the obstinate resistance of some unbelievers to the beliefs and ideals of Islam.

Ibn 'Abbās, and others said that God's words *"strive with the utmost endeavor"* denote the duty of preaching and exhortation as the greatest of all kinds of Jihād. Ibn Abbas said that "with it" refers to the Holy Qur'ān.[6] The Jihād here considered as most essential by Ibn 'Abbās, cousin and associate of the Prophet 🙼 and foremost exegete of the Qur'ān, is the call to the Word of God—the Jihād of Education.

IMĀM MALIK BIN ANAS

Imām Malik bin Anas stated in *al-Mudawwanat al-kubra:*[7]

The first of what God has sent His Messenger 🙼 is to call people to Islam without fighting. He did not give him permission to fight nor to take money from people. The Prophet 🙼 stayed like

---

[6] Muhammad Sa'īd R. Al-Būtī, Jihad fil-islām, Dar al-Fikr., Beirut, 1995, p. 16.

[7] Imām Mālik bin Anas, *al-Mudawwanat al-kubra,* p.180.

that for thirteen years in Makkah, bearing all kinds of persecutions, until he left for Madīnah.

IBN QAYYIM AL-JAWZĪYYAH

Ibn Qayyim al-Jawzīyyah says in *Zād al-ma'ād*:

God commanded the Jihād of Education when He revealed:

وَلَوْ شِئْنَا لَبَعَثْنَا فِي كُلِّ قَرْيَةٍ نَذِيرًا فَلَا تُطِعِ الْكَافِرِينَ وَجَاهِدْهُم بِهِ جِهَادًا كَبِيرًا

If We willed, We could raise up a warner in every village. Therefore listen not to the Unbelievers, but strive against them with the utmost strenuousness, with the (Qur'ān). [25: 51, 52]

This is a Makkan Chapter, therefore God command therein the Jihād of the non-Muslims by argumentation, elocution and conveying the Qur'ān.[8]

IMĀM NAWAWĪ

Imām Nawawī, in his book *al-Minhaj*, when defining Jihād and its different categories, said:

> . . . one of the collective duties of the community as a whole (*farḍ kifāyah*) is to lodge a valid protest, to solve problems of religion, to have knowledge of Divine Law, to command what is right and forbid wrong conduct.[9]

IMĀM AD-DARDĪR

The explanation of Jihād in Imām ad-Dardīr's book *Aqrab al-Masālik* is that it is propagating the knowledge of the Divine Law, commending right and forbidding wrong. He emphasized that it is not permitted to skip this category of Jihād and implement the combative form, saying, "the first [Islamic] duty is

---

[8] Ibn Qayyim al-Jawzīyyah, Zād al-Ma'ād.

[9] al-Nawawī, *al-Minhāj*, p. 210.

to call people to enter Islam, even if they had been preached to by the Prophet ﷺ beforehand."[10]

IMĀM BAHŪTĪ

Similarly, Imām Bahūtī commences the chapter on Jihād in his book *Kashf al-Qina'* by showing the injunctions of collective religious duties *(kifāyah)* that the Muslim Nation must achieve before embarking on combative Jihād. These include preaching and educating about the religion of Islam, dismissing all the uncertainties about the religion and making available all the skills and qualifications which people might require to meet their religious, material and physical needs, as these constitute the regulations of both this life and the life to come. Hence, *da'wah* is the cornerstone of the "building" of Jihād, and any attempt to build without this "stone" would damage the integrity of the Jihād.[11]

DR. SA'ĪD RAMĀDĀN AL-BŪTĪ

Al-Būtī says in his book *al-Jihād fil-Islām* states:

> The most significant category of Jihād was the one established simultaneously with the dawn of the Islamic *da'wah* at Makkah. This was the basis for the other resulting kinds accorded with the situations and circumstances.[12]

> Clarifying the image of Islam, removing all misconceptions and stereotypes held by non-Muslims and building a trusting relationship by working with them in ways that accord with their way of thinking are all primary forms of Educational Jihād. Similarly, establishing a strong community and nation which can fulfill all the needs of its people, thereby creating for them the conditions in which the message

---

[10] Imām al-Dardīr, *Al-Sharh al-saghīr.*

[11] Mansūr bin Yunes al-Bahūtī, *Kashf al-qina'a,* p. 33.

[12] *Jihād fil-islām,* Muhammad Sa'īd R. Al-Būtī, Dar al-Fikr, Beirut, 1995, p. 16.

can be heard are therefore requirements of Jihādic. These effort fulfill the Qur'ānic injunction:

$$وَلْتَكُن مِّنكُمْ أُمَّةٌ يَدْعُونَ إِلَى الْخَيْرِ وَيَأْمُرُونَ بِالْمَعْرُوفِ وَيَنْهَوْنَ عَنِ الْمُنكَرِ وَأُوْلَٰئِكَ هُمُ الْمُفْلِحُونَ$$

Let there arise out of you a band of people inviting to all that is good, enjoining what is right, and forbidding what is wrong: and these it is that shall be successful. [3:104]

Until this is accomplished, the preconditions of combative Jihād remain unfulfilled.[13]

YŪSUF AL-QARADĀWĪ

The popular yet controversial Islamic scholar, Shaykh Yūsuf al-Qaradāwī, said:

Jihād is an obligation on everyone, but not killing and fighting.

Citing Ibn Qayyim's work on the topic, he states:

Whoever looks into the sources as to the understanding of Jihād, will see that one can be a mujāhid, but it is not necessary to be a combatant; that is only when combat is forced on you by the invasion of your country.

SAYYID SĀBIQ

Sayyid Sābiq, in his renowned work *Fiqh as-Sunnah* says:

God sent His Messenger ﷺ to all of mankind and ordered him to call to guidance and the religion of truth. While he dwelled in Makkah, he called to God by using wisdom and the best exhortation. It was inevitable for him to face opposition from his people who saw the new message as a danger to their way of life. It

---

[13] *Musnad* Ahmad. Similar ahādith are narrated in Abū Dawūd and Tirmidhī.

was through the guidance of God that he faced the opposition with patience, tolerance and forbearance. God says:

$$وَاصْبِرْ لِحُكْمِ رَبِّكَ فَإِنَّكَ بِأَعْيُنِنَا$$

So wait patiently (O Muhammad) for thy Lord's decree, for surely thou art in Our sight [52:48]

$$فَاصْفَحْ عَنْهُمْ وَقُلْ سَلَامٌ فَسَوْفَ يَعْلَمُونَ$$

Then bear with them (O Muhammad) and say: Peace. But they will come to know [43:89]

$$فَاصْفَحِ الصَّفْحَ الْجَمِيلَ$$

So forgive, O Muhammad, with a gracious forgiveness [15: 85]

Here we see that God does not permit the fighting of evil with evil, or to wage war on those who fight opposing the message of Islam nor to kill those who cause discord to the Muslims. And He said:

$$ادْفَعْ بِالَّتِي هِيَ أَحْسَنُ فَإِذَا الَّذِي بَيْنَكَ وَبَيْنَهُ عَدَاوَةٌ كَأَنَّهُ وَلِيٌّ حَمِيمٌ$$

Nor can goodness and Evil be equal. Repel (Evil) with what is better: Then will he between whom and thee was hatred become as it were thy friend and intimate! [41:34]

As the persecution continued, it became harder and harder to bear, reaching its peak when the Quraysh conspired against the life of the Noble Messenger ﷺ. At this time, it became imperative that he migrate from Makkah to Madīnah, both for his personal safety, for the very survival of the new faith, and in an effort to avoid war. Thus thirteen years after the commencement of Qur'ān's revelation, the Prophet ﷺ ordered his companions to emigrate to Madīnah.

It is clear then that the Prophet ﷺ did not try to repulse the aggressive attacks against the Muslims by his tribesmen, but sought to avoid conflict and avoid their persecution by means of migration.

ESTABLISHMENT OF THE ISLAMIC NATION/STATE

Sayyid Sābiq continues:

وَإِذْ يَمْكُرُ بِكَ الَّذِينَ كَفَرُوا لِيُثْبِتُوكَ أَوْ يَقْتُلُوكَ أَوْ يُخْرِجُوكَ وَيَمْكُرُونَ وَيَمْكُرُ اللَّهُ وَاللَّهُ خَيْرُ الْمَاكِرِينَ

And when those who disbelieve plot against thee (O Muhammad) to wound thee fatally, or to kill thee or to drive thee forth; they plot, but God (also) plotteth; and God is the best of plotters [8:30]

Madīnah thus became the new capital of Islām. As a nation-state for the Muslims, and their new home, an entirely new political situation had evolved. Whereas before the Muslims had been a persecuted minority with no land or political base, upon establishing Madīnah as a nation ruled by the legislation of Islam, and a sanctuary to which new Muslims under persecution could flee, it was imperative to protect this homeland from the aggressive designs of the enemy, who sought nothing less than the complete extirpation of the Muslim faith and killing of its adherents. Thus, when the enemies opened war against them the situation of the Muslims became gravely dangerous, taking them to the brink of destruction at the hands of the enemy, in which case the very message was in danger of being lost. [14]

So Jihād in its combative sense did not come about until after the Prophet ﷺ and his Companions were forced to leave their country and hometown of Makkah, fleeing for safety to in Madīnah after thirteen years of propagating the call to the faith and calling for freedom of belief. God said:

---

[14] Sayyid Sabiq, *Fiqh as-Sunnah*, 2nd ed., vol. 3, (Beirut: Daru'l-Fikr, 1980).

ثُمَّ إِنَّ رَبَّكَ لِلَّذِينَ هَاجَرُواْ مِن بَعْدِ مَا فُتِنُواْ ثُمَّ جَاهَدُواْ وَصَبَرُواْ إِنَّ رَبَّكَ مِن بَعْدِهَا لَغَفُورٌ رَّحِيمٌ

*But verily thy Lord,- to those who leave their homes after trials
and persecutions, - and who thereafter strive and struggle [for the
faith] and patiently persevere, - Thy Lord, after all this is oft-
forgiving, Most Merciful. [16:110]*

So we see that, after the migration to Madīnah, God described
Jihād as a struggle to patiently endure through persecution and trial.

In Madīnah, the Prophet's message became the basis for a model
constitution for civic society and social life. This is borne out by the
emphasis the Prophet ﷺ made on caring for the poor, the emancipation of
slaves, giving rights to women and building a civic society by levying taxes on
the rich to benefit the poor, establishing community centers and communal
homes in which people could meet. He was able to establish a nation-state
based on freedom of speech and freedom of religion, where all faiths flourished
without conflict.

In establishing this society in Madīnah, the Prophet ﷺ sought to keep his
new nation safe, just as today every country has security as a dominant
concern. Therefore he built up an army of his followers to keep his borders safe
from any enemy attack. In particular, they were under great threat due to the
Prophet's ﷺ teaching opposing the hegemony of tyrants.

FIRST LEGISLATION OF COMBATIVE JIHĀD

Even then, the legislation to fight was not made until the Makkans set
out to eliminate the newly established Islamic nation, by raising an
army and setting forth with the intention of assaulting and destroying
the community in Madīnah.

Sayyid Sābiq continues:

The first verse revealed regarding fighting was:

أُذِنَ لِلَّذِينَ يُقَاتَلُونَ بِأَنَّهُمْ ظُلِمُوا وَإِنَّ اللَّهَ عَلَى نَصْرِهِمْ لَقَدِيرٌ الَّذِينَ أُخْرِجُوا مِن دِيَارِهِم بِغَيْرِ حَقٍّ إِلَّا أَن يَقُولُوا رَبُّنَا اللَّهُ وَلَوْلَا دَفْعُ اللَّهِ النَّاسَ بَعْضَهُم بِبَعْضٍ لَهُدِّمَتْ صَوَامِعُ وَبِيَعٌ وَصَلَوَاتٌ وَمَسَاجِدُ يُذْكَرُ فِيهَا اسْمُ اللَّهِ كَثِيرًا وَلَيَنصُرَنَّ اللَّهُ مَن يَنصُرُهُ إِنَّ اللَّهَ لَقَوِيٌّ عَزِيزٌ الَّذِينَ إِن مَّكَّنَّاهُمْ فِي الْأَرْضِ أَقَامُوا الصَّلَاةَ وَآتَوُا الزَّكَاةَ وَأَمَرُوا بِالْمَعْرُوفِ وَنَهَوْا عَنِ الْمُنكَرِ وَلِلَّهِ عَاقِبَةُ الْأُمُورِ

Sanction is given unto those who fight because they have been wronged; and God is indeed able to give them victory; Those who have been driven from their homes unjustly only because they said: Our Lord is God. For had it not been for God's repelling some men by means of others, cloisters and churches and oratories and mosques, wherein the name of God is oft mentioned, would assuredly have been pulled down. Verily God helpeth one who helpeth Him. Lo! God is Strong, Almighty. Those who, if We give them power in the land, establish worship and pay the poor due and enjoin kindness and forbid iniquity. And God's is the sequel of events. [78: 39-40]

This verse shows that permission for fighting was granted for three reasons:

1) They were oppressed by their enemies and expelled by them from their homes unjustly for no reason except that they practiced the religion of God and said, "Our Lord is God." They then came under the obligation to take back the country from which they had been expelled.

2) Where not for God's permission for this type of defense, all places of worship, (including churches, synagogues and mosques) would have been destroyed in which the name of God was remembered (see page 26 for a more detailed explanation of this aspect) because of the oppression of those who aggressively opposed belief.

3) The goal of victory was to establish the freedom of religion, to establish the prayer, to give charity, to command the good and to forbid what is disliked.

This last justification also means that, as long as preaching and practice are not prohibited, the Muslims cannot fight. Thus, a Jihād against a country in which Muslims freely practice their religion and are allowed to teach Islam would be impermissible.

In the second year after the Migration, God ordered the Muslims to fight by saying:

كُتِبَ عَلَيْكُمُ الْقِتَالُ وَهُوَ كُرْهٌ لَكُمْ وَعَسَى أَن تَكْرَهُوا شَيْئًا وَهُوَ خَيْرٌ لَكُمْ وَعَسَى أَن تُحِبُّوا شَيْئًا وَهُوَ شَرٌّ لَكُمْ وَاللَّهُ يَعْلَمُ وَأَنتُمْ لَا تَعْلَمُونَ

Warfare is ordained for you, though it is hateful unto you; but it may happen that ye hate a thing which is good for you, and it may happen that ye love a thing which is bad for you. God knoweth, ye know not. [2: 216]

This verse shows that, in general, warfare was disliked. Despite this, it was called for at times when the security of the nation was threatened by external belligerency.

Thus, with a simple studious examination of the relevant verses, we discover that there were two different kinds of Jihād: that of Makkah and that of Madīnah. The one in Makkah was primarily focused on education. In Madīnah, Jihād was by two methods: education and fighting, though only after the enemies attacked the Prophet ﷺ within his own city-state. Additionally, the Muslims who had been expelled invoked the right to return to their homeland, and if opposed to use force.

Combative Jihād was authorized only after the Prophet ﷺ migrated along with his followers from Makkah to Madīnah, having been persecuted and finally expelled from their country, fleeing from persecution and torture. Their condition was not unlike those of many people today, who flee persecution in their home countries, becoming refugees in foreign nations. Many are welcomed in these nations as al-Ansār of Madīnah welcomed al-

Muhājirūn, sharing with them all they possessed of their wealth and their homes.

Thus Madīnah became the first city for the believers in which the new message, Islam, was established and they sought to keep it safe. Just as all nations do today, they built up an army and weaponry. And, just as in the modern world, they were obliged to respond and repel those who attacked them.

Thus, the majority of Muslims scholars including Imām Abū Hanifa, Imām Mālik and Imām Ahmad ibn Hanbal say that combative Jihād is to defend oneself and to attack the aggressors.

IS ISLAM BY NATURE HOSTILE TO NON-MUSLIMS?

The idea, often postulated in the media, that Islam is hostile to non-Muslims simply because they are not Muslims is a major a misconception. According to the majority of scholars, there is no inherently valid reason to hold any hostility towards them. Sayyid Sābiq says:

The relationship of Muslims with non-Muslims is one of acquaintance, cooperation, righteousness and justice for God says:

يَا أَيُّهَا النَّاسُ إِنَّا خَلَقْنَاكُم مِّن ذَكَرٍ وَأُنثَى وَجَعَلْنَاكُمْ شُعُوبًا وَقَبَائِلَ لِتَعَارَفُوا إِنَّ أَكْرَمَكُمْ عِندَ اللَّهِ أَتْقَاكُمْ إِنَّ اللَّه عَلِيمٌ خَبِيرٌ

O mankind! We created you from a single (pair) of a male and a female, and made you into nations and tribes, that ye may know each other (not that ye may despise (each other). Verily the most honored of you in the sight of God is (he who is) the most righteous of you. And God has full knowledge and is well acquainted (with all things). [49:13]

109

LOYALTY AND ENMITY (*AL-WALA WAL-BARA'A*)

Many of today's self-appointed Islamic leaders and scholar's state:

"Enmity for the sake of God (al-barā'a) means to declare opposition in deed, to take up arms against His enemies . . ."[15]

Sayyid Sābiq says:

This meaning does not permit prevention of friendship with the non-Muslims. The prohibition exists [only] when friendship with the non-Muslims is meant in aggression against the Muslims. Serious dangers to the existence of Islam come from assisting the non-Muslims who are [actively] working against the Muslims, weakening the power [and security] of the believing society.

As far as the relationship between the Muslims and non-Muslim subjects (*dhimmis*) living in Muslim nations, harmony, peace, with good manners and courtesy, friendly social intercourse, mutual welfare and cooperation for the sake of righteousness and good conscience are all that Islām calls for.

Even with regard to those who fought against the Muslims, despite their enmity, God says:

عَسَى اللَّهُ أَن يَجْعَلَ بَيْنَكُمْ وَبَيْنَ الَّذِينَ عَادَيْتُم مِّنْهُم مَّوَدَّةً وَاللَّهُ قَدِيرٌ وَاللَّهُ غَفُورٌ رَّحِيمٌ

It may be that God will grant love (and friendship) between you and those whom ye (now) hold as enemies. For God has power (over all things); And God is Oft-Forgiving, Most Merciful. [60:7]

---

[15] Muhammad Sā'īd al-Qahtānī , *Al-Walā wal-Barā'*, Translated by Omar Johnstone.

RELIGIOUS FREEDOM OF NON-MUSLIMS

It is a right for the People of the Book to practice the laws of their religion, judges and courts, enforcing those rules among themselves. Their churches or temples are not to be demolished, nor are their crosses or other religious symbols to be broken. The Messenger of God ﷺ said:

اتركوهم وما يدينونه

"Leave them to what they worship."

Additionally, it is the right of a Christian or Jewish spouse of a Muslim to attend her church or temple. Her husband has no right to prevent her from going.

Islām permits those of other faiths the foods that their religion allows. Swine are not killed because of them, nor is their wine destroyed as long as it is permitted to them. Therefore, they have more latitude than the Muslims, who are prohibited from drinking wine and eating pork.

They also have the freedom to follow their own laws of marriage, divorce and charity, and to conduct these affairs as they wish without any conditions or limits.

Their honor and rights are under the protection of Islām, and they are given the right of deliberation and discussion within the limits of reason and decorum, as long as they respect the rights of others, practice good conduct and avoiding rudeness and harshness. God says:

وَلَا تُجَادِلُوا أَهْلَ الْكِتَابِ إِلَّا بِالَّتِي هِيَ أَحْسَنُ إِلَّا الَّذِينَ ظَلَمُوا مِنْهُمْ وَقُولُوا آمَنَّا بِالَّذِي أُنزِلَ إِلَيْنَا وَأُنزِلَ إِلَيْكُمْ وَإِلَٰهُنَا وَإِلَٰهُكُمْ وَاحِدٌ وَنَحْنُ لَهُ مُسْلِمُونَ

And dispute ye not with the People of the Book, except with means better (than mere disputation), unless it be with those of them who inflict wrong (and injury): but say, "We believe in the revelation which has come down to us and in that which came

down to you; Our God and your God is one; and it is to Him
we bow (in Islam)." [29:46]

وَإِنْ أَحَدٌ مِّنَ الْمُشْرِكِينَ اسْتَجَارَكَ فَأَجِرْهُ حَتَّى يَسْمَعَ كَلاَمَ اللهِ ثُمَّ أَبْلِغْهُ مَأْمَنَهُ ذَلِكَ بِأَنَّهُمْ قَوْمٌ لاَّ يَعْلَمُونَ

If one amongst the Pagans ask thee for asylum, grant it to him,
so that he may hear the word of God; and then escort him to
where he can be secure. That is because they are men without
knowledge. [9:6]

These verses also show that, even if unbelievers come to the
Muslims seeking to live and work in their nation for any reason, the
Muslims must grant them safety and security to demonstrate the great
care and compassion of Islam. Again, this emphasizes the point that
combative Jihād is only waged against aggressors.

According to some schools of jurisprudence, the punishments for
Muslims and non-Muslims are the same, except for those things
permitted to non-Muslims by their faith, such as drinking wine or
eating pork.

Islām makes lawful eating what the People of the Book slaughter
and Muslim men are permitted to marry their women, for God says:

الْيَوْمَ أُحِلَّ لَكُمُ الطَّيِّبَاتُ وَطَعَامُ الَّذِينَ أُوتُوا الْكِتَابَ حِلٌّ لَّكُمْ وَطَعَامُكُمْ حِلٌّ لَهُمْ وَالْمُحْصَنَاتُ مِنَ الْمُؤْمِنَاتِ
وَالْمُحْصَنَاتُ مِنَ الَّذِينَ أُوتُوا الْكِتَابَ مِن قَبْلِكُمْ إِذَا آتَيْتُمُوهُنَّ أُجُورَهُنَّ مُحْصِنِينَ غَيْرَ مُسَافِحِينَ وَلاَ
مُتَّخِذِي أَخْدَانٍ . . .

This day are (all) things good and pure made lawful unto you.
The food of the People of the Book is lawful unto you and yours
is lawful unto them. (Lawful unto you in marriage) are (not
only) chaste women who are believers, but chaste women among
the People of the Book, revealed before your time,- when ye give
them their due dowers, and desire chastity, not lewdness, nor
secret intrigues ... [5:5]

Islām sanctions visiting and counseling their sick, offering them guidance and dealing with them in business. It is established that when the Messenger of God ﷺ passed to his Lord, his armor was given as credit for a debt from a Jew.

In another case, when some of the Companions sacrificed a sheep, the Prophet ﷺ said to his servant, "Give this to our Jewish neighbor."

It is obligatory for the leader of the Muslims (caliph) to protect those of the People of the Book who are in Muslim lands just as he would Muslims, and to seek the release of those of them who are captured by the enemy.

The Messenger of God ﷺ forbade killing a covenanter when he said:

مَنْ قَتَل مُعَاهِداً، لَمْ يَرِحْ رَائِحَةَ الْجَنَّة

The one who kills a covenanter will not smell the fragrance of paradise.[16]

It can be truly said that, in Arab and Muslim nations, the Christians, the Jews and all other non-Muslims are in fact covenanters, for they pay their taxes supporting the nation's standing army. Given this, it is the duty of the ruler to protect their safety. The concept of a covenant of protection, while not explicitly spelled out today, is fulfilled through government taxation.

FORCED CONVERSION?

We have seen above that the foundation of Jihād is Islamic propagation (*da'wah*). The question is often asked whether Islam condones forced conversion of non-Muslims. This is the image sometimes projected by Western scholars, but it is wrong. The Qur'ān clearly states:

لاَ إِكْرَاهَ فِي الدِّينِ قَد تَّبَيَّنَ الرُّشْدُ مِنَ الْغَيِّ

---

[16] Ibn Mājah reported it in his *Sunan*, from ʿAbd-Allāh bin ʿAmr.

*There is no compulsion in religion, the path of guidance stands
out clear from error* [2:256] *and* [60:8].

In this verse, the word *rushd*, or "path of guidance," refers to the
entire domain of human life, not just to the rites and theology of
Islam.

There is no debate about the fact that pre-Islamic Arabia was a
misguided society dominated by tribalism and a blind obedience to
custom. In contrast, the clarity of Islam and its emphasis on reason
and rational proofs obviated any need to impose it by force. This verse
is a clear indication that the Qur'ān is strictly opposed to the use of
compulsion in religious faith. Similarly, God addressed the Prophet ﷺ
saying:

فَذَكِّرْ إِنَّمَا أَنتَ مُذَكِّرٌ

Remind them, for you are only one who reminds. [88:21]

God also addresses the believers, urging them to obey the
injunctions of Islam:

وَأَطِيعُواْ اللَّهَ وَأَطِيعُواْ الرَّسُولَ وَاحْذَرُواْ فَإِن تَوَلَّيْتُمْ فَاعْلَمُواْ أَنَّمَا عَلَى رَسُولِنَا الْبَلَاغُ الْمُبِينُ

*Obey God, and obey the Messenger, and beware (of evil): if you
do turn back, then know that it is Our Messenger's duty to
proclaim (the message) in the clearest manner.* [5:92]

However, this verse makes it clear that the Messenger's ﷺ duty is
only to proclaim and preach the message; it remains to each individual
to accept and to follow.

As for forced conversion, no reliable evidence exists that Muslims
ever intended or attempted to impose the specific rites and beliefs of
Islam on anyone. The histories of Central Asia, Spain, India, the
Balkans and all of Southeast Asia are concrete proof of this.

ISLAM'S HISTORY OF GOOD-TREATMENT OF NON-MUSLIMS

Indeed, it is well established in history that when People of the Book were persecuted in non-Muslim lands, they would often seek refuge with the leader of the Muslims (caliph), and this refuge was not refused. A well-known example of this is that of the Jews in Andalusia who, after it was conquered by the Spanish and taken from the hands of the Muslim Moors in 1492, faced the infamously cruel Inquisition. Jews and Muslims had no choice but to flee their homes, convert to Catholicism or die. The Jews sought the protection of Sultan Suleyman, the ruler of the Ottoman Empire and caliph of the Muslims, and asylum was granted to them. For this reason, one finds a sizable population of Jews in Istanbul, which was seat of the Ottoman Empire at that time.

DOES ISLAM CALL FOR ONGOING WAR AGAINST NON-MUSLIMS?

Some Orientalists as well as some radical interpreters of Islam, assert that Islām condones an ongoing combative Jihād, that it calls for a continual war upon the non-Muslims until they repent and accept Islam or else pay the poll-tax. However, the majority of Muslims scholars reject this view, citing as evidence:

وَإِنْ أَحَدٌ مِنَ الْمُشْرِكِينَ اسْتَجَارَكَ فَأَجِرْهُ حَتَّى يَسْمَعَ كَلَامَ اللهِ ثُمَّ أَبْلِغْهُ مَأْمَنَهُ ذَلِكَ بِأَنَّهُمْ قَوْمٌ لَا يَعْلَمُونَ

...and if anyone of the polytheists seeks your protection then grant him protection, so that he may hear the Word of God, and then escort him to where he can be secure, that is because they are men who know not. [9:6][17]

The Imams argued from this that as long as the condition that they are submissive and willing to live peacefully among the believers

---

[17] The singular exception to this consensus being the opinion of Imām Shafi'i.

our divine obligation is to treat them peacefully, despite their denial of Islam. The succeeding verse:

فَمَا اسْتَقَامُوا لَكُمْ فَاسْتَقِيمُوا لَهُمْ إِنَّ اللَّهَ يُحِبُّ الْمُتَّقِينَ

So long as they are true to you, stand you true to them. Verily! God loved those who fear God. [9:7]

This verse instructs the Muslims to observe treaty obligations with meticulous care, and not to break them unless the other side breaks them first.

Based on the clear arguments of the scholars from the Qur'ān and Hadith, the majority concluded that fighting is not a permanent condition against unbelievers, but only when treaties are broken or aggression has been made against Muslim territory (*dār al-Islām*) by unbelievers.

On the other hand, educating non-Muslims about Islam *is* a continuous Jihād, as is made clear by the agreed-upon, mass-transmitted hadith:

عن ابي هريرة، عن رسول الله صلى الله عليه وسلم قال: "امرت ان اقاتل الناس حتى يشهدوا ان لا اله الا الله . . .

The Messenger of God ﷺ said, "I have been ordered to fight the people until they declare that there is no god but God and that Muhammad is His Messenger, establish prayers, and pay zakat . . ."[18]

In his book *al-Jihād fil-Islam*, Dr. Sa'īd Ramadān Būtī explains this hadith in detail based on the understanding of the majority of jurists, showing that linguistically the word "fight" here and in many other places does not refer to combat, rather to struggle, including in

---

[18] A mass-transmitted hadith narrated by Bukhārī, Muslim, Abū Dawūd, Tirmidhī, an-Nasā'ī, Ibn Majah from Abū Hurayrah.

its scope *da'wah*, preaching, exhortation and establishment of the state apparatus whereby Islamic preaching is protected. It does not mean forcing anyone to become Muslim at the point of a sword, and numerous examples can be cited from the life history of the Prophet ﷺ showing he never forced conversion, nor did his Successors.

Dr. Būtī explains that the linguistic scholars of hadith showed that the word *uqātil* أقَاتِـــل used by the Prophet ﷺ means "fight" and not *aqtul* أقتـــل "kill". In Arabic, this word is used in terms of defending against an attacker or an oppressor, it is not used to mean attack or assail.

In light of this, Dr. Būtī shows that this hadith connotes:

I have been ordered by God to fulfill the task of calling people [peacefully] to believe that God is One and to defend [against] any aggression against this divine task, even though this defense requires fighting aggressors or enemies.[19]

Dr. Būtī explains that this hadith is reminiscent of a saying by the Prophet ﷺ on the occasion of the Treaty of Hudaybiyyah where he told his mediator, Badil ibn Warqa:

وإن هم أبوا فوالذي نفسي بيده لأقاتلنهم على أمري هذا حتّى تنفرد سالفتي ولينفذن الله أمره

"But if they do not accept this truce, by God in whose Hands my life is, I will fight with them, defending my Cause till I get killed."[20]

By these words, Badil ibn Warqa was tasked with inviting the Quraysh to peace, and simultaneously, warning of the ongoing war that had already exhausted them. Dr. Būtī remarks:

The Prophet's ﷺ words "I will fight with them defending my Cause," in this context certainly means that he, while inclining to peace with the enemy,

---

[19] Muhammad Sa'īd R. Al-Būtī, *Jihād fil-islām*, Dar al-Fikr, Beirut, 1995, p. 58.

[20] Bukhārī.

would react to their combative aggression in the same way, if they had insisted on their aggression.[21]

Note also that in the years after the Treaty was signed, it was the Quraysh who violated it. Near the end of the seventh year after migration, the Quraysh—along with the allied Banī Bakr tribe—attacked the Banī Khuzaʿah tribe, who were allies of the Muslims. The Banī Khuzaʿah appealed to the Prophet ﷺ for help and protection.

The Banī Khuzaʿah sent a delegation to the Prophet ﷺ requesting his support. Despite this provocation and clear violation of the treaty, the Prophet ﷺ avoided acting in haste to renew hostilities. Instead he sent a letter to the Quraysh demanding payment of blood money for those killed, and an end to their alliance with the Banī Bakr. Otherwise, the Prophet ﷺ said, the treaty would be declared null and void.

The Quraysh then sent an envoy to Medina to announce that they considered the Treaty of Hudaybīyyah null and void. However, they immediately regretted this step. Therefore, the leader of the Quraysh, Abū Sufyān, himself traveled to Madīnah to renew the contract. Despite having been the greatest enemy of the Muslims, and despite the Quraysh already being in violation of the pact they had solemnly entered into, no hand was laid on this Qurayshi chief—someone who infamous for his persecution and harm to Muslims in Makkah. He was even permitted to enter the Prophet's ﷺ mosque and announce his desire to reinstate the treaty.

From this, one can argue that if the state of unbelief were a sufficient pretext for war, then the Prophet ﷺ would have been warranted in seizing Abū Sufyān and initiating hostilities against the Quraysh then and there. However, on the contrary, Abū Sufyān came and went from Madīnah freely and only after some time were the hostilities renewed based on the Makkans aggressive violation of the pact.

---

[21] al-Būtī, *Op. cit.*

God says:

...وَقَاتِلُوا الْمُشْرِكِينَ كَافَّةً كَمَا يُقَاتِلُونَكُمْ كَافَّةً وَاعْلَمُوا أَنَّ اللَّهَ مَعَ الْمُتَّقِينَ

...and fight the mushrikūn, [polytheists Pagans] all together as they fight you all together. But know that God is with those who restrain themselves. [9:36]

Here we understand *"fight the unbelievers collectively as they fight you collectively"* means "treat them in the same way as they treat you." Commenting on this, Dr. Būtī says, "You should deal with the unbelievers kindly and equitably, unless they are rampant and out to destroy us and our faith. Hence the motive for [combative] Jihād becomes self-defense."[22]

Finally God says:

فَإِنِ اعْتَزَلُوكُمْ فَلَمْ يُقَاتِلُوكُمْ وَأَلْقَوْا إِلَيْكُمُ السَّلَمَ فَمَا جَعَلَ اللَّهُ لَكُمْ عَلَيْهِمْ سَبِيلاً

So, if they hold aloof from you and wage not war against you and offer you peace, God alloweth you no way against them. [4: 90]

We see here an explicit statement from God, that it is not permitted to fight with those who are not engaged in belligerency, despite their being non-believers.

CONDITIONS FOR COMBATIVE JIHĀD

The ruler of the Muslims, the Imām, is completely answerable to the people and their legal apparatus, the most important representatives of which are the scholars. Islam establishes strict conditions that must be satisfied before a Muslim ruler can declare combative Jihād. The position of the law is that combative Jihād can only be declared at such a time when it can be reasonably proven that:

---

[22] al-Būtī, *Op. cit.*, p. 92.

- there are aggressive designs against Islam

- there are concerted efforts to eject Muslims from their legally acquired property

- military campaigns are being launched to destroy them

PRE-CONDITION: LEADERSHIP

Saʿīd Ramādān al-Būtī, in *Jihād in Islam,* says:

> It is known that Islamic Shariʿah rules can be divided into two groups: first the Communicative Rules (Ahkām at-Tablīgh) that inform you of how to behave in your life, including all matters of worship and daily life, and second, the Rules of Leadership (*Ahkām al-Imāmah),* which are related to the judicial system, the Imām or leader.

> The Rules of Leadership are those rules that have been directed from the leader to the citizens. In the time of the Prophet ﷺ, he was leader, so this applied to anything directed from himself to the Muslims. After the Prophet ﷺ, such directives became the responsibility of the caliph, his successor. This means the Imām of the Muslims is the leader of every Muslim nation. He is the person responsible for the application of the rules as he sees fit. These rules are flexible within the geographical, societal and cultural norms of the nation, which the leader can exercise by God's Grace, to apply them for the benefit of all the people.

> Declaring combative Jihād is the topmost responsibility of the Imām. He is the only responsible body that can declare the time and place of Jihād, lead it or terminate its mission. It is in no way the responsibility of individual Muslims to declare Jihād without the order of the leader. Note in this regard the ʿulama are not in the position to issue a call for combative Jihād.

There are two kinds of combative Jihād. One is the combative Jihād to fight a nation which aggresses against a Muslim nation, under the orders of the Imām, or leader. The second category of combative Jihād, which is called *as-sa'il*, means the fight against an assailant, attacker or violator. We will not go into this aspect as it falls under the Communicative Rules, not the Rules of Imamate. This is based on the hadith related by 'Abdullāh ibn 'Umar, in which the Prophet ﷺ said, "He who is killed in defense of his belongings or in self-defense or in defense of his religion is a martyr."[23]

The category *as-sa'il* refers to someone defending his private possessions as when someone attacks him at home or his business in order to steal, to harm, or out of hatred due to differences of religion. This does not come under the aspect of Imāmah, where nations are involved.[24]

IBN QUDĀMA

It is an essential pre-condition that there be a leader of the Muslims, an Imām, to declare combative Jihād. In *al-Mughni*, Ibn Qudāma, a respected scholar of the Hanbali school, states:

> *Declaring Jihād is the responsibility of the ruler and is His independent legal judgment. And it is the duty of the citizens to obey whatever he regards appropriate.*[25]

AL-DARDĪR

Al-Dardīr says: "proclaiming Jihād comes through the Ruler's assignment of a commander."[26]

---

[23] Narrated by Abū Dawūd, ibn Majah, Tirmidhī, and Ahmad.

[24] al-Būtī, *Op. cit.,* pp. 108-109.

[25] Ibn Qudāma, *Al-Mughni*, Vol. 9, p. 184.

AL-JAZĀʾIRĪ

Abū Bakr Al-Jazāʾirī states that the pillars of combative Jihād are:

A pure intention, and that it is performed behind a Muslim Ruler and beneath his flag and with his permission ... And it is not allowed for them to fight without a Ruler because Allāh says:

يَا أَيُّهَا الَّذِينَ آمَنُوا أَطِيعُوا اللَّهَ وَأَطِيعُوا الرَّسُولَ وَأُوْلِي الأَمْرِ مِنكُمْ

O ye who believe! Obey God, and obey the Messenger, and those charged with authority among you. [4:59][27]

AL-TAHANŪĪ

According to *Kashf al-Qina'a* by al-Tahanūī:

Ordering combative Jihād is the responsibility of the Imām and his legal judgment (ijtihād) because he is the most knowledgeable about the enemy's status and their nearness or farness, their intention and conspiracy.[28]

MAWARDĪ

Mawardī, a Shafi'ite authority, while enumerating the obligations of a Muslim ruler says:

His sixth obligation is to conduct [combative] Jihād against those who show hostility against Islam ...[29]

---

[26] al-Dardīr, *Al-Sharh al-Saghīr*, Vol. 2, p. 274.

[27] Abū Bakr's al-Jazā`irī, *Minhāj al-Muslim*, Chapter of Jihād.

[28] 28 al-Tahanūī, *Kashf al-Qina'a*, vol. 3, p. 41.

[29] 29 Abū'l-Hasan 'Alī Mawardī, *al-Ahkām al-sultānīyyah*, 1st ed., (Beirut: Daru'l-Kitab al-'Arabi, 1990), p. 52.

AL-SARKHASĪ

Al-Sarkhasī, in *al-Mabsūt,* said:

The Ruler of the Muslims must, in most cases, exert all efforts to lead an army himself or dispatch a military detachment of Muslims; and trust in God to aid him in achieving victory.[30]

ASH-SHARBĪNĪ

Ash-Sharbīnī said:

Collective-duty Jihād becomes applicable when the Imām fortifies the frontiers, reinforces the fortresses and ditches, and arms his military leaders. It also applies when the Imām or his deputies take the lead of the army ... [31]

SAYYID SĀBIQ

The principle that only the ruler of the Muslims can declare combative Jihād is so explicit and categorical that all the scholars of this Ummah unanimously uphold it. Sayyid Sābiq, referring to this consensus, writes:

Among *kifāyah* obligations, there is a category for which the existence of a ruler is necessary e.g., [combative] Jihād and administration of punishments.[32]

ZAFAR AHMAD 'UTHMĀNĪ

Zafar Ahmad 'Uthmānī, a Hanafite jurist writes:

---

[30] Al-Sarkhasī, *al-Mabsūt*, vol. 10, p. 3.

[31] Al-Sharbīnī, *Mughnī al-muhtāj*, vol. 4, p. 210.

[32] Sayyid Sābiq, *Fiqh as-Sunnah*, 2nd ed., vol. 3, (Beirut: Daru'l-Fikr, 1980), p. 30. cited by Shehzad Saleem in "No Jihad without a State," Renaissance Monthly, December 1999.

It is obvious from the hadith narrated by Makhūl[33] that Jihād becomes obligatory with the ruler who is a Muslim and whose political authority has been established either through nomination by the previous ruler similar to how Abū Bakr transferred the reins [of his Khilāfah to 'Umar] or through pledging of allegiance by the *ulama* or a group of the elite ... In my opinion, if the oath of allegiance is pledged by *ulama* or by a group of the elite to a person who is not able to guard the frontiers and defend honor [of the people] organize armies or implement his directives by political force nor is he able to provide justice to the oppressed by exercising force and power, then such a person cannot be called "Amir" (leader) or "Imām" (ruler). He, at best, is an arbitrator and the oath of allegiance is at best of the nature of arbitration and it is not at all proper to call him "Amir" or an "Imām" in any [official] documents, nor should the people address him by these designations ... It is not imperative for the citizens to pledge allegiance to him or obey his directives, and no [combative] Jihād can be waged alongside him.[34]

IMĀM FARĀHĪ

In the words of Imām Farāhī:

---

[33] The complete text of the Hadith is:

حدثنا أحمد بن صالح حدثنا ابن وهب حدثني معاوية بن صالح عن العلاء بن الحارث عن مكحول عن أبي هريرة قال

قال رسول الله صلى الله عليه وسلم الجهاد واجب عليكم مع كل أمير برا كان أو فاجرا والصلاة واجبة عليكم خلف كل مسلم برا كان أو فاجرا وإن عمل الكبائر

والصلاة واجبة على كل مسلم برا كان أو فاجرا وإن عمل الكبائر

Makhūl narrates from Abū Hurayrah who narrates from the Prophet ﷺ: "Jihad is obligatory upon you with a Muslim ruler whether he is pious or impious, and the prayer is obligatory upon you behind every Muslim whether he is pious or impious even if he is guilty of the major sins." (*Sunan Abū Da'ud*, No. 2171)

[34] Zafar Ahmad 'Uthmani, *Ii'la al-Sunan*, 3rd ed., vol. 12, (Karachi: Idaratu'l-Qur'an wa 'Ulumi'l-Islamiyyah, 1415 AH), pp. 15-16. Cited by Shehzad Saleem in "No Jihad without a State," *Renaissance Monthly*, December 1999.

If [combative] Jihād is not waged by a person who holds political authority, it amounts to anarchy and disorder.[35]

AL-ALBĀNĪ

The Salafi scholar Al-Albānī, stressing the necessity of Jihād being established by the ruler of the Muslims, said:

In the present time there is no Jihād in the Islamic land, while undoubtedly there is combat taking place in numerous places but there is no Jihād, established under a solely Islamic banner that abides by Islamic legislation.

These represent only a sampling of many quotes from scholars regarding combative Jihād. They suffice to demonstrate the responsibility of the Imamate in ordering it. The actual title, whether he be called Imām, caliph, king or president, is not important – his position as ruler is what counts. The leader is the one who has been elected to administer the foreign policy of his nation, and has been entrusted by the people to conduct the common affairs of the state, sign treaties, forbid wrong deeds, suppress criminals, fight aggressors, and settle people down in their homes and the like.

In light of this, we must ask ourselves today, "Where is the Caliph of Muslims in the present time?" Since there is no caliphate the fundamental requirement of leadership does not exist. So, while there still is combat between one nation and another, it is no longer considered to be Jihād as that term is defined in Islamic law.

The leadership of the Muslims can never devolve to a group of people living in a country who come against its government. The aforementioned rulings of the scholars and the many verses of Qur'ān and Hadith citation invalidate the methods of the so-called "Islamic parties" who establish states within the state and act as if they are the rightful rulers of Muslims. Their methodology is to initiate war by

---

[35] Cited by Shehzad Saleem in "No Jihad without a State," Renaissance Monthly, December 1999.

attacking non-Muslims in their country or other countries, and they do this without the permission of the Muslim rulers or the Muslim nation and without the consensus of its scholars. The result is that everyone suffers from the disastrous consequences of their actions (This subject is discussed in detail on page 40).

SELF-DEFENSE

Every community has the right to self-defense and, in the case of Islam, where religion is the primary dimension of human existence, war in defense of the nation becomes a religious act. A lack of understanding of this quality of Islam, its non-secularism; has also contributed considerably to the fear that, when Islam speaks about war it means war to convert others to Islam. This might be true of other faiths, but Islam must be allowed to speak for itself.

Al-Dardīr says of this:

Jihād becomes a duty when the enemy takes [Muslims] by surprise.[36]

Saʿīd Ramadān al-Būtī shows that fighting in this case is an obligation of the community as a whole:

عن سعيدِ بن زيدٍ قال: سمعتُ رسُولَ اللهِ صلَّى اللهُ عليهِ وسلَّم يقول: "من قُتِل دونَ مالِهِ فهو شهيدٌ. ومن قُتِل دونَ دمِهِ فهو شهيدٌ. ومن قُتِل دونَ دينِهِ فهو شهيدٌ."

This is based on the Prophet's ﷺ saying:

He who is killed in defense of his belongings, or in self-defense, or for his religion, is a martyr.[37]

Muslims are enjoined to act kindly and justly towards members of other faiths except in two circumstances: firstly, if they dispossess

---

[36] al-Dardīr, *Al-Sharh al-Saghīr*, Vol. 2, p. 274.

[37] Abū Dawūd and Tirmidhī.

Muslims of their legitimate land-rights, and secondly, if they engage in hostilities towards Muslims by killing or attacking them, or show clear intent to do so (*al-hirābah*) because of their religion. In the second eventuality, it is the duty of the Muslim ruler to declare combative Jihād as a defensive action to repel such attacks.

It is evident from the Qur'ān and other sources that the armed struggle against the polytheists was legislated in the context of specific circumstances after the Prophet ﷺ had migrated from Makkah to Madīnah. There he secured a pact with the Jewish and Arab tribes of the city, who accepted him as the leader of their community. In the milieu of this newly-founded base of operations, under the governance of divine legislation and the leadership of the Prophet ﷺ, Islam attained the status of a nation with its co-requisite territory and the accompanying need to protect its self-interests. At that time, the divine command was revealed permitting Jihād, but this occurred only after:

- Persistent refusal of the Makkan leadership to allow the practice of Islam's religious obligations, specifically to perform the Hajj at Makkah (Note that, despite this belligerency, the Prophet ﷺ agreed to a truce).

- Continuous, unabated persecution of Muslims remaining at Makkah after the Prophet's emigration to Madīnah triggered an armed insurrection against Qurayshite interests in the Hijaz.

- Makkans themselves commencing a military campaign against the Muslims at Madīnah with the sole objective of eradicating Islam.

- Key security pledges being abrogated unilaterally by a number of tribes allied to the Prophet ﷺ, forcing him into a dangerously vulnerable position.

These conditions for defensive Jihād involving armed struggle were then clearly specified in the Qur'ān:

وَقَاتِلُواْ فِي سَبِيلِ اللهِ الَّذِينَ يُقَاتِلُونَكُمْ وَلَا تَعْتَدُواْ

And fight in the way of God those who fight against you, and do not transgress [limits] for God likes not the transgressors [2:190]

Explaining this verse, Sayyid Sābiq states:

This verse also consists of prohibiting aggression due the fact that God does not love aggression. This prohibition is not abrogated by any verse and is a warning that aggression is devoid of God's love. Verses that consist of such warnings are not abrogated, because aggression is tyranny and God never loves tyranny. Therefore, a legal war is justified only when it is to prevent discord and harm to the Muslims and for them to have the freedom to practice and live according to their religion.[38]

God says:

أَلَا تُقَاتِلُونَ قَوْمًا نَّكَثُواْ أَيْمَانَهُمْ وَهَمُّواْ بِإِخْرَاجِ الرَّسُولِ وَهُم بَدَؤُوكُمْ أَوَّلَ مَرَّةٍ

"Will you not fight a people who have violated their oaths and intended to expel the Messenger while they did attack you first?" [9:13]

The clear picture that emerges here is that the command to fight was given in relation to specific conditions. God said:

أُذِنَ لِلَّذِينَ يُقَاتَلُونَ بِأَنَّهُمْ ظُلِمُوا وَإِنَّ اللَّهَ عَلَى نَصْرِهِمْ

To those against whom war is made, permission is given (to fight), because they are wronged;- and verily, God is most powerful for their aid; [22:39]

---

[38] Sayyid Sābiq, *Fiqh as-Sunnah.*

Expulsion

The Qur'ān then goes on to describe the conditions of those who are permitted to fight:

وَمَا لَنَا أَلَّا نُقَاتِلَ فِي سَبِيلِ اللّٰهِ وَقَدْ أُخْرِجْنَا مِن دِيَارِنَا وَأَبْنَائِنَا

They said: "How could we refuse to fight in the cause of God, seeing that we were turned out of our homes and our families?" [2: 246]

الَّذِينَ أُخْرِجُوا مِن دِيَارِهِم بِغَيْرِ حَقٍّ إِلَّا أَن يَقُولُوا رَبُّنَا اللّٰهُ وَلَوْلَا دَفْعُ اللّٰهِ النَّاسَ بَعْضَهُم بِبَعْضٍ لَّهُدِّمَتْ صَوَامِعُ وَبِيَعٌ وَصَلَوَاتٌ وَمَسَاجِدُ يُذْكَرُ فِيهَا اسْمُ اللّٰهِ كَثِيرًا وَلَيَنصُرَنَّ اللّٰهُ مَن يَنصُرُهُ إِنَّ اللّٰهَ لَقَوِيٌّ عَزِيزٌ

(They are) those who have been expelled from their homes in defiance of right,- (for no cause) except that they say, "our Lord is God". Did not God check one set of people by means of another, there would surely have been pulled down monasteries, churches, synagogues, and mosques, in which the name of God is commemorated in abundant measure. God will certainly aid those who aid his (cause);- for verily God is full of Strength, Exalted in Might, (able to enforce His Will). [22:40]

Denial of Religious Freedom

In later times, the Muslims engaged in warfare to establish the "Pax Islamica," or Islamic Order. The legal and political order must flow from the divine imperative. It alone guarantees the rights of every individual by keeping in check all the dark psychic tendencies of man, preventing him from indulging in anti-social behaviors ranging from political aggression to the most common criminal act. It is for this reason that the Qur'ān calls on the believers to go forth in defense of those whose rights and liberty have been trampled by the unbridled tyranny of oppressors and conquering armies, or who are prevented from freely hearing the word of God espoused to them by preachers and educators. God says:

وَمَا لَكُمْ لاَ تُقَاتِلُونَ فِي سَبِيلِ اللهِ وَالْمُسْتَضْعَفِينَ مِنَ الرِّجَالِ وَالنِّسَاءِ وَالْوِلْدَانِ الَّذِينَ يَقُولُونَ رَبَّنَا أَخْرِجْنَا مِنْ هَذِهِ الْقَرْيَةِ الظَّالِمِ أَهْلُهَا وَاجْعَل لَنَا مِن لَدُنْكَ وَلِيًّا وَاجْعَل لَنَا مِن لَدُنْكَ نَصِيرًا

"How should ye not fight for the cause of God and of the feeble among men and of the women and the children who are crying: Our Lord! Bring us forth from out this town of which the people are oppressors! Oh, give us from Thy presence some protecting friend! Oh, give us from Thy presence some defender!" [4:75]

This verse gives two explanations for fighting:

1. Fighting in the cause of God, until discord has vanished and the religion is practiced freely for God alone. This means one cannot fight a Jihād against a country in which Muslims can freely practice their religion and teach Islam to others.

2. Fighting for the sake of the weak, such as those who converted to Islām in Makkah, but were unable to undertake the migration to Madīnah. The Quraysh tortured them until they prayed to God for liberation. They had no means of protection from the persecution of the oppressors.

God permitted armed Jihād against an aggressor, where He said:

إِنَّ اللهَ اشْتَرَى مِنَ الْمُؤْمِنِينَ أَنفُسَهُمْ وَأَمْوَالَهُم بِأَنَّ لَهُمُ الْجَنَّةَ يُقَاتِلُونَ فِي سَبِيلِ اللهِ فَيَقْتُلُونَ وَيُقْتَلُونَ وَعْدًا عَلَيْهِ حَقًّا فِي التَّوْرَاةِ وَالإِنجِيلِ وَالْقُرْآنِ وَمَنْ أَوْفَى بِعَهْدِهِ مِنَ اللهِ فَاسْتَبْشِرُوا بِبَيْعِكُمُ الَّذِي بَايَعْتُم بِهِ وَذَلِكَ هُوَ الْفَوْزُ الْعَظِيمُ

Lo! God hath bought from the believers their lives and their wealth because the Garden will be theirs: they shall fight in the way of God and shall slay and be slain. It is a promise which is binding on Him in the Torah and the Gospel and the Qur'ān. [9:111]

This demonstrates that the rule of repelling aggression is not specifically for Muslims, but is the role of anyone following the Torah and the Gospel—the right to fight those who attack them. Giving one's self in God's Way, means repelling the aggressor. *"A promise binding on Him in truth"* means God took it on Himself as a right, not only in the Qur'ān, but also in the Torah and the Gospel, giving the believers the Garden of Paradise in exchange for their selves and their lives.

He said, *"God bought from the believers their lives and their wealth."* This also means to give one's wealth for building up society, for the welfare of others, for establishing hospitals, school and civic society.

CAN MUSLIMS FIGHT IF RELIGIOUS PRACTICE IS NOT PREVENTED?

God said:

لَا يَنْهَاكُمُ اللَّهُ عَنِ الَّذِينَ لَمْ يُقَاتِلُوكُمْ فِي الدِّينِ وَلَمْ يُخْرِجُوكُم مِّن دِيَارِكُمْ أَن تَبَرُّوهُمْ وَتُقْسِطُوا إِلَيْهِمْ إِنَّ اللَّهَ يُحِبُّ الْمُقْسِطِينَ

God forbids you not, with regard to those who fight you not for (your) Faith nor drive you out of your homes, from dealing kindly and justly with them: for God loveth those who are just.

God only forbids you, with regard to those who fight you for (your) Faith, and drive you out of your homes, and support (others) in driving you out, from turning to them (for friendship and protection). It is such as turn to them (in these circumstances), that do wrong. [60:8,9]

One sees here that God does not hinder the Muslims from dealing justly and kindly with those who do not fight them for their religion. Today we see that Muslims reside in many non-Muslim nations, and are living in peace, observing all their religious obligations and are free to practice their faith. One cannot find any nation in which mosques are forced to close, or the authorities are banning the Qur'ān or other religious books, or Muslims are prevented from praying, paying their poor-due, fasting or attending the pilgrimage. Instead we find that all Muslims today are free to practice their faith in every nation, around the globe.

$$فَاحْكُم بَيْنَهُم بِالْقِسْطِ إِنَّ اللَّهَ يُحِبُّ الْمُقْسِطِينَ$$

Surely God loves those who are just. [5:42]

Islam urges the believers to practice goodness with those who are doing good to them, and thus they are not permitted to attack them.

POSSIBILITY OF SUCCESS

Jihād against countries who are guilty of oppression and persecution only becomes compulsory after all political negotiations have failed and it becomes clear that the enemy is set on aggression. Additionally, the Muslims may fight only when there is a likelihood of success. The state must prepare whatever is necessary of weapons, materials and men, for God says:

$$وَأَعِدُّواْ لَهُم مَّا اسْتَطَعْتُم مِّن قُوَّةٍ$$

Make ready for them all thou canst of (armed) force [8:40]

This means the leader must spend to the utmost of the nation's ability and expend every effort to arm the Muslims for battle, for it is God's rule that without strength you cannot fight. To recklessly do so without the possibility of success would result only in killing one's self and killing one's people and the creation of mayhem (*fitnah*), which may be worse than killing. God says:

$$وَالْفِتْنَةُ أَشَدُّ مِنَ الْقَتْلِ$$

for tumult and oppression (fitnah) are worse than slaughter;
[2:191]

Mayhem might lead to crimes against innocent people. That is why God said it is worse than killing. *Fitnah* is the work of *munāfiqīn*, hypocrites. It refers here to conspiracy, the result of which may be a great war instigated between one or more nations, which may result in the death of thousand or millions of innocents.

الآنَ خَفَّفَ اللهُ عَنكُمْ وَعَلِمَ أَنَّ فِيكُمْ ضَعْفًا فَإِن يَكُن مِنكُم مِّئَةٌ صَابِرَةٌ يَغْلِبُوا مِئَتَيْنِ وَإِن يَكُن مِّنكُم أَلْفٌ يَغْلِبُوا أَلْفَيْنِ بِإِذْنِ اللهِ وَاللهُ مَعَ الصَّابِرِينَ

Now God has lightened your [task] for He knows that there is weakness among you. So if there are of you a hundred steadfast person, they shall overcome two hundred, if there are a thousand of you, they shall overcome two thousand with the leave of God and God is with the patient. [8:66]

God here declared that if the ratio of Muslim warriors to their opponents is one to two (1:2), they may fight and they will be given Divine Support in an open fight facing the enemy directly, warrior-to-warrior. This was a reduction from the original ratio, in which the believers were obligated to fight even if the ratio of Muslims to their opponents was one to ten (1:10).

How, then, can a small group declare combative Jihād against an entire nation, when the group possesses no more than a few dozen or a few hundred dedicated warriors? If it is not permitted for 19 people to fight a group in excess of 38, what about instigating war against a massively fortified and armed nation of over 250 million? This is, in reality nothing more than an invitation to mayhem. The result is the endangerment of the entire Muslim Ummah. It is nothing but confusion, sedition and disorder, and the Prophet ﷺ declared those who create turmoil to be under God's curse:

The Prophet ﷺ said:

Confusion/sedition/mayhem (fitnah) is dormant. God curses the one who rouses it.

Today's radicals justify combative Jihād without state authority by citing the skirmishes carried out by one of the Muslim converts against the Makkans. An article in Pakistan's *Renaissance* magazine by Shehzad Saleem explains:

We know from history that after the treaty of Hudaybiyyah, Abū Basīr defected to Madīnah. According to the terms of the treaty he was duly returned back to the Quraysh by the Prophet ﷺ. He was sent back in the custody of two people of the Quraysh. He killed one of his two custodians and again defected to Madīnah. When he arrived in Madīnah, the Prophet ﷺ was angry with what he had done. Sensing that the Prophet ﷺ would once again return him to the Quraysh, he left Madīnah and settled at a place near Dhu'l-Marwah, where later on other people joined home. From this place, they would attack the caravans of the Quraysh.

If these guerrilla attacks are analyzed in the light of the Qur'ān, the basic thing which comes to light is that whatever Abū Basīr and his companions were doing was not sanctioned at all by Islam. The Qur'ān says that the actions and deeds of a person who has not migrated to Madīnah are not the responsibility of an Islamic state:

وَالَّذِينَ آمَنُوا وَلَمْ يُهَاجِرُوا مَا لَكُمْ مِنْ وَلَايَتِهِمْ مِنْ شَيْءٍ حَتَّى يُهَاجِرُوا

And as to those who believed but did not migrate [to Madīnah], you owe no duty of protection until they migrate. [8:72]

Not only did the Qur'ān acquit the newly founded Islamic state of Madīnah from the actions of these people, we even find the following harsh remarks of the Prophet ﷺ about Abū Basīr when he returned to Madīnah after killing one of his two custodians:

وَيْلُ أُمِّهِ مِسْعَرَ حَرْبٍ لَوْ كَانَ لَهُ

His mother is unfortunate! Though he has the right, he is going to ignite the flames of war.[39]

WHO IS INVOLVED IN COMBAT?

COMMUNAL OBLIGATION

Combative Jihād is not an obligation on every individual among the Muslims, rather it's an communal obligation (*fard kifāyah*) fulfilled when some take on the duty to repel the enemy. God says:

وَمَا كَانَ الْمُؤْمِنُونَ لِيَنفِرُوا كَافَّةً فَلَوْلَا نَفَرَ مِن كُلِّ فِرْقَةٍ مِّنْهُمْ طَائِفَةٌ لِّيَتَفَقَّهُوا فِي الدِّينِ وَلِيُنذِرُوا قَوْمَهُمْ إِذَا رَجَعُوا إِلَيْهِمْ لَعَلَّهُمْ يَحْذَرُونَ

And the believers should not all go out to fight. Of every troop of them, a party only should go forth, that they (who are left behind) may gain sound knowledge in religion, and that they may warn their folk when they return to them, so that they may beware [9: 122]

We see from this verse that combative Jihād is not for everyone. If a group of people have been assigned to undertake combative Jihād by their leader, the rest must not go. Rather, their duty is to stay behind and study, in order to educate themselves and others. So, even when combative Jihād has been called for, both those who go forth to combat and those who stay behind to develop understanding of religion are participants in Jihād. This verse makes it clear that those who stay behind and study religion are equal to those who go forth to battle, by saying: "their duty is to stay behind and study, in order to educate themselves and to educate others."

---

[39] Bukhārī.

In this verse, God emphasized that not all the believers should go out to fight. This indicates that there is a decision to be made: who will go fight and who will not? Mu'adh ibn Jabal related:

Acquire knowledge because doing so is goodness, seeking it is worship, reviewing it is glorifying God and researching it is Jihād...[40]

From this, we can see that learning the religion becomes more important than participation in battle, for in doing so one learns the beliefs and rulings that all Muslims must follow in this life. Understand these rulings, including those related to Jihād, is essential and can only be accomplished by study and education.

CONSCRIPTION

The same verse shows that, from every group, only a party of them goes forth. That means the army is to be taken from different citizens from various parts of the country, *"from every group of them,"* and today means volunteers or recruits who have been assigned and trained go forth to fight, while the rest of the citizens remain behind to train and educate themselves.

Participation in combative Jihād becomes obligatory for an individual when he is ordered by the leader to be present in the line of fire. Hence the Messenger of God ﷺ said:

لَا هِجْرَةَ، وَلَكِنْ جِهَادٌ وَنِيَّةٌ، وَإِذَا اسْتُنْفِرْتُمْ فَانْفِرُوا

There is no migration (after the opening of Makkah), but Jihād and good intention. So when you are called to go forth in stopping aggression, then do so.[41]

---

[40] Imām Ibn Rajab al-Hanbalī, *Warathatu'l-Anbiyā'*. Chapter 8, pgs. 37-38.

[41] Bukhārī reported it from Ibn 'Abbās.

This means that when you are called up by your leader you must obey, as that is part of obedience to God, the Prophet ﷺ and those in authority. Along with this, it is incumbent on any group who seek to fight as soldiers in the way of God against aggression by unbelievers, to firstly pledge themselves to their leader, who organizes the army. Thereafter, they organize their ranks and prepare them to fight.

Setting forth when called is <u>mandatory</u> on Muslims, provided they are:

- Male

- In possession of sound reason

- Have attained the age of maturity

- Healthy

In addition, his family must possesses sufficient funds to meet their needs until he completes the duty assigned him by the leader.

الَّذِينَ لاَ يَجِدُونَ مَا يُنفِقُونَ حَرَجٌ إِذَا نَصَحُواْ لِلّهِ وَرَسُولِهِ لَيْسَ عَلَى الضُّعَفَاء وَلاَ عَلَى الْمَرْضَى وَلاَ عَلَى

Not unto the weak nor unto the sick nor unto those who can find naught to spend is any fault (to be imputed though they stay at home) if they are true to God and His messenger [9: 91]

This verse means there is no obligation on those who have a weak personality, or a radical mentality nor on those who have no talent to go forth for war. Only those persons selected by the ruler or his appointed leaders should go forth, not those who might commit rash actions because of excessive emotional zeal, nor those who are mentally ill and might commit crimes like bombings, suicide attacks and so forth.

As Ibn Qayyim al-Jawzīyyah said in *Zād al-maʿād*:

The Prophet ﷺ said:

المجاهد من جاهد نفسه في طاعة الله والمهاجر من هجر الخطايا والذنوب

The fighter is the one who fights himself in obedience to God and the one who emigrates is the one who emigrates from iniquities.[42]

The Jihād of the self is a prerequisite over the Jihād of the enemy in the open and initial basis for it.

Without a doubt, the one who does not fight his self is not allowed to make combative Jihād against the external enemy. How is it possible for him to fight his [external] enemy, when his own enemy, which is right beside him, dominates over him and commands him? So, as he did not wage war on the [internal] enemy of God, it is even more impossible for him to set out against the enemy until he fights himself.[43]

لَيْسَ عَلَى الْأَعْمَى حَرَجٌ وَلَا عَلَى الْأَعْرَجِ حَرَجٌ

There is no blame for the blind, nor is there blame for the lame, nor is there blame for the sick (that they go not forth to war). [29: 17]

SURPRISE ATTACK

When the enemy suddenly arrives in a place which the Muslims reside, it is obligated for the inhabitants to go out and fight them. No one is exempt from this obligation.

AGE REQUIREMENT

Ibn 'Umar said, "I was presented to the Messenger of God ﷺ at the time of the battle of Uhud when I was fourteen years of age, and he did not give me permission to fight."

This is because Jihād is not obligated except on the one who has reached the appropriate age.

---

[42] Ahmad recorded it in his *Musnad*, from Fadālah bin Ubayd.

[43] Ibn Qayyim al-Jawīyyah, *Zād al-Ma'ād.*

JIHĀD OF WOMEN

'Ā'isha asked, "O Messenger of God ﷺ, is Jihād obligated for women?" He said, "Jihād without fighting. Hajj and 'Umrah [are their Jihād]."[44]

God says:

وَلَا تَتَمَنَّوْا مَا فَضَّلَ اللَّهُ بِهِ بَعْضَكُمْ عَلَى بَعْضٍ لِلرِّجَالِ نَصِيبٌ مِّمَّا اكْتَسَبُوا وَلِلنِّسَاء نَصِيبٌ مِّمَّا اكْتَسَبْنَ وَاسْأَلُوا اللَّهَ مِن فَضْلِهِ إِنَّ اللَّهَ كَانَ بِكُلِّ شَيْءٍ عَلِيمًا

And covet not the thing in which God hath made some of you excel others. Unto men a fortune from that which they have earned, and unto women a fortune from that which they have earned. (Envy not one another) but ask God of His bounty. Lo! God is ever Knower of all things [4:32]

It is reported by 'Ikrimah that some women inquired about Jihād and other women said, "We wish that God grant us a portion of the reward the military expeditions receive from the reward of what the men share."

This does not prevent women from going out to treat the wounded.

It is reported that the Prophet ﷺ was out on a military expedition and Umm Salīm was with him and other women from the al-Ansār. They were giving water to the fighters and treating the wounded.[45]

PARENTS' PERMISSION

In the case of a major, obligatory combative Jihād, the parents' permission is not required, but as far as the voluntary combative Jihād,

---

[44] Related by Muslim and Bukhārī.

[45] Muslim, Abū Dawūd and at-Tirmidhī.

their permission is a must. If one parent has passed away, permission from the other suffices.

Ibn Mas'ūd related:

I asked the Messenger of God ﷺ which action is most loved to God and he said, "Prayer in its time. Then I said, "then what," and he said, "Being good to your parents." Then I said, "what after that?" He said, "Jihād in the way of God."[46]

Ibn 'Umar said:

A man came to the Prophet ﷺ and asked permission for combative Jihād and he said, "Are not your parents alive?" He said, "Yes." Then he said, "Then ask them first, then fight."[47]

One does not go out in Jihād unless he has provided for the needs of his family and the service of his parents. This is the prerequisite of Jihād; even more, it is the best Jihād.

JIHĀD BETWEEN MUSLIMS

Properly speaking Jihād, in the case of internal dissension, only occurs when two conditions are met and the Muslims fight in support of the Imām against the offending parties: a just leader fighting an unjustifiable insurrection. In Islam, allegiance and obedience to a *just* authority is obligatory.

It must be noted also that rebellions against authority—and especially political authority, simply for the sake of rebellion—have no place in the concept of Jihād. In this age of relativism, the spirit of rebellion seems to have penetrated every layer of society. However, Islam and its principles cannot be made subservient to these cultural trends.

---

[46] Muslim and Bukhārī recorded it.

[47] Bukhārī, Abū Dawūd, and an-Nisā'ī. at-Tirmidhī graded it sound.

In some of the contemporary "Islamic" groups, Jihād has been distorted into something resembling a Marxist or socialist concept of class revolt aimed at overthrowing the authority of the state. In the often fervently materialistic milieu of contemporary political and revolutionary ideologies, Islam is inevitably reduced to nothing more than a social philosophy. This reductionism reflects an abysmal misunderstanding of the essential function of Islam, which is to turn the "face" of the human receptacle away from the world of disharmony and illusion to the tranquility and silence of divine awareness and vision. Inward Jihād, as we alluded to at the beginning of this presentation, has a key role to play in this respect.

SEEKING PEACE

The ruler, the political leader of the whole country, has the power to ratify peace treaties consistent with the interests of the Muslims.

God said:

$$يَا أَيُّهَا الَّذِينَ آمَنُوا ادْخُلُوا فِي السِّلْمِ كَافَّةً وَلَا تَتَّبِعُوا خُطُوَاتِ الشَّيْطَانِ$$

Enter into peace completely and do not follow the steps of Satan. [2:208]

And:

$$وَإِن جَنَحُوا لِلسَّلْمِ فَاجْنَحْ لَهَا وَتَوَكَّلْ عَلَى اللهِ إِنَّهُ هُوَ السَّمِيعُ الْعَلِيمُ$$

And if they incline to peace, incline thou also to it, and trust in God. [8: 60]

Sayyid Sābiq states:

This verse is the command to accept peace when the enemy accepts it, even if their acceptance is known beforehand to be deception and deceit.[48]

God says:

وَقَاتِلُوهُمْ حَتَّى لاَ تَكُونَ فِتْنَةٌ وَيَكُونَ الدِّينُ لِلّهِ فَإِنِ انتَهَوْا فَلاَ عُدْوَانَ إِلاَّ عَلَى الظَّالِمِينَ

And fight them on until there is no more tumult or oppression, and there prevail justice and faith in God; but if they cease, Let there be no hostility except to those who practice oppression. [2:193]

From this verse we see that fighting is exhorted until oppression is ended. With the words, *"but if they cease,"* God legislates that once justice prevails and no one is prevented from observing their belief in God, then fighting should end. God grants that arms be set aside, *"except to those who practice oppression."*

وَقَاتِلُوهُمْ حَتَّى لاَ تَكُونَ فِتْنَةٌ وَيَكُونَ الدِّينُ كُلُّهُ لِلَّه فَإِنِ انتَهَوْا فَإِنَّ اللَّهَ بِمَا يَعْمَلُونَ بَصِيرٌ

And fight them on until there is no more tumult or oppression, and there prevail justice and faith in God altogether and everywhere; but if they cease, verily God doth see all that they do. [8:39]

Thus, peace is not only permitted, but called for after the adversary, even if still inimical, ceases its aggression. However, precaution and watchfulness is not to be abandoned in this situation, for here God reminds the Muslims of His Own Attribute, *"verily God doth see all that they do."*

After establishing the Islamic state in Madīnah, the Prophet ﷺ said that the way of the Muslims is one. No single group can autonomously declare war or fight, nor can any one group make peace

---

[48] Sayyid Sābiq, *Fiqh as-Sunnah.*

by itself. Rather, the entire country must make peace. When a peace treaty is made by the country's leader, all subjects of that country are bound by that decision, regardless of whether the leader was appointed or elected. The final decision is up to the ruler, after consultation with others.

If a state has no leader, then it must select one. Otherwise, its interests will be represented internationally by neighboring states. Those nations can come together and agree on a treaty with any foreign country on its behalf. This applies as much in peace as it does in war.

TAXATION

Ibn Qudāma said that a treaty of peace involves agreeing with combatant non-Muslims to end hostilities for a period of time, whether or not it involves paying a tax. He asserted that Muslims are allowed to make peace treaties that do not require non-Muslims to pay a tax, because the Prophet ﷺ of God did so on the occasion of the Hudaybīyya Treaty. Ibn Qudāma says that Imām Ahmad gave this opinion, as did Imām Abū Hanifa.[49]

CONDUCT OF COMBAT

PROHIBITION OF KILLING NON-COMBATANTS

Islam prohibits utterly the killing of those who are not actual military personnel.

حدثنا عثمان بن أبي شيبة حدثنا يحيى بن آدم وعبيد الله بن موسى عن حسن بن صالح عن خالد بن الفزر حدثني أنس بن مالك أن رسول الله صلى الله عليه وسلم قال انطلقوا باسم الله وبالله وعلى ملة رسول الله ولا تقتلوا شيخا فانيا ولا طفلا ولا صغيرا ولا امرأة ولا تغلوا وضموا غنائمكم وأصلحوا وأحسنوا إن الله يحب المحسنين ﴿ وَأَحْسِنُوا إِنَّ اللَّهَ يُحِبُّ الْمُحْسِنِينَ ﴾

---

[49] Ibn Qudāma, *al-Mughni*, vol. 12, pp. 691-693.

The Prophet ﷺ sent the following message to his military leaders who were setting forth in the way of Jihād to stop hostile advances and defend Muslim territories:

Advance in the name of God, with God, on the pattern of the Messenger of God ﷺ. That means do not to kill the elderly, infants or children and women. Do not exceed the proper bounds. Gather your spoils and make peace "and do good. Lo! God loveth those who do good." [2:195][50]

حدثني أبي عن جده حدثنا أبو الوليد الطيالسي حدثنا عمر بن المرقع بن صيفي بن رباح بن رباح قال

رباح بن ربيع قال

رجلا فقال مع رسول الله صلى الله عليه وسلم في غزوة فرأى الناس مجتمعين على شيء فبعث كما قال وعلى المقدمة خالد لتقاتل هذه كانت ما انظر علام اجتمع هؤلاء فجاء فقال على امرأة قتيل فقال لخالد لا يقتلن امرأة ولا عسيفا بن الوليد فبعث رجلا فقال قل

The Prophet ﷺ passed by a woman who was killed and said, "She was not engaged in fighting." The Prophet ﷺ then sent to the Muslim leader Khālid ibn al-Walīd the following message, "The Prophet ﷺ orders you not to kill women or servants."[51]

This is clear evidence the woman was not a fighter and the Prophet ﷺ prohibited her killing. From the strong expression the Prophet ﷺ made, going so far as to send a letter to his topmost military commander, we see how concerned he was to prevent such incidents and to insure that every single Muslim warrior was aware of the rules of combat.

The question arises here: When someone explodes a bomb or commits a suicide attack in a public place, how many innocent women, children and elderly people are killed? If one woman's death caused the Prophet ﷺ to scold his top general, Khālid ibn al-Walīd,

---

[50] Abū Dawūd narrated it in his *Sunan* from Anas bin Mālik.

[51] Narrated in the *Sunan* of Abū Dāwūd from Rābih ibn Rabi', and At-Tabārī narrated a similar tradition in his *al-Awsat* from Ibn 'Umar. Similar narrations are related in Ibn Mājah, and Ahmad from Hanzalah.

what then about killing twenty, thirty or even hundreds of non-combatants, some of whom may even be Muslim?

Just as the Messenger of God ﷺ forbade the killing of women and the young, he forbade killing priests.

The first caliph Sayyidina Abū Bakr as-Siddīq's commandment to the leader of the first Islamic military expedition after the Prophet ﷺ included the following injunction:

No hermit should be molested. Only those should be killed who take up arms against you.[52]

We see from these various narrations—and there are many more like them—that the Prophet ﷺ prohibited the Muslims to kill anyone, Muslim or non-Muslim, if they are not active transgressors against the security of the nation.

This shows that terrorist acts, in particular suicide attacks which kill indiscriminately, are utterly unacceptable forms of combat, even during valid combat authorized for defense of the nation.

One of Islam's fundamental principles is the sanctity of life. There is simply no way in Islam to justify the killing of innocents, even as a form of mass retribution, which many radicals today use as justification for their large-scale attacks on civilians. Islam prohibits blood feud and specifies retribution only towards the one who committed a crime.

God says:

$$ \text{وَلَا تَقْتُلُوا النَّفْسَ الَّتِي حَرَّمَ اللهُ إِلَّا بِالْحَقِّ} $$

Slay not the life which God has made sacrosanct unless it be in a just cause. [6:151]

---

[52] Cited in *Tārīkh aṭ-Ṭabarī*, vol. 3, pp. 226-227.

وَمَن يَقْتُلْ مُؤْمِنًا مُّتَعَمِّدًا فَجَزَآؤُهُ جَهَنَّمُ خَالِدًا فِيهَا وَغَضِبَ اللّهُ عَلَيْهِ وَلَعَنَهُ وَأَعَدَّ لَهُ عَذَابًا عَظِيمًا

And whoever kills a believer intentionally, his recompense is Hell to abide therein, and the Wrath and the Curse of God are upon him, and a great punishment is prepared for him, [4:93]

Since no one can say for sure "this person is not a believer," it becomes forbidden to kill any human being without just cause.

PROHIBITION OF BURNING THE ENEMY

الزناد حدثني محمد بن حدثنا سعيد بن منصور حدثنا مغيرة بن عبد الرحمن الحزامي عن أبي حمزة الأسلمي عن أبيه

فخرجت فيها وقال إن وجدتم فلانا أن رسول الله صلى الله عليه وسلم أمره على سرية قال بالنار يعذب لا فإنه تحرقوه ولا إن وجدتم فلانا فاقتلوه فأحرقوه بالنار فوليت فناداني فرجعت إليه فقال النار رب إلا

It is prohibited to burn the enemy with fire because the Messenger ﷺ said, "Kill [the enemy] but do not burn him. For no one punishes with fire except the Lord of the Fire."[53]

This hadith illustrates the Prophet's emphasis on mercy and avoidance of harm when he established such laws of conduct on the battlefield. Only in modern times were rules of warfare, such as the Geneva Conventions which make it impermissible to kill or torture prisoners of war, adopted worldwide. Yet, 1400 years ago, the Prophet ﷺ established detailed rules of warfare in which even using fire in combat was prohibited, going far beyond the restrictions modern nations have been willing to accept.

According to this hadith, weapons of fire are not approved by God. God prohibited burning, yet the majority of attacks by Islamic groups today involve bombs and explosions, such as the attacks on the

---

[53] Abū Dawūd narrated it in his *Sunan*, from Muhammad bin Hamzah al-Aslamī from his father.

World Trade Center on September 11, 2001, in which 3,000 people were incinerated.

PROHIBITION OF MUTILATING THE DEAD

قال عمران بن حصين كان رسول الله صلى الله عليه وسلم يحثنا على الصدقة وينهانا عن المثلة

Imrān bin Husayn said the Messenger of God ﷺ encouraged us to give charity and forbade us from mutilation.[54]

PROHIBITION OF DESPOILING

Abū Bakr as-Siddīq commanded the leader of the first Islamic military expedition after the Prophet ﷺ, saying:

No fruit-bearing trees are to be cut down and no crops should be set on fire. No animal should be killed except those slaughtered for eating. Only those should be killed who take up arms against you.[55]

SUICIDE ATTACKS

Suicide itself is specifically prohibited in Islam. God said:

وَلَا تَقْتُلُوا أَنفُسَكُمْ إِنَّ اللَّهَ كَانَ بِكُمْ رَحِيمًا

Kill yourselves not, for God is truly merciful to you. [4:29]

and:

وَلَا تُلْقُوا بِأَيْدِيكُمْ إِلَى التَّهْلُكَةِ وَأَحْسِنُوا

Throw not yourselves into the mouth of danger. [2:195]

---

[54] Narrated in Bukhārī.

[55] Cited in *Tārikh at-Tabarī*, vol. 3, pp. 226-227.

These verses establish the general principle that killing oneself is forbidden. Thus, Islam utterly forbids suicide. On this the Prophet ﷺ said:

عن عمران بن حصين قال: قال رسول الله صلى الله عليه وسلم"من قتل نفسه بشيء في الدنيا عذب به في الآخرة."

Whoever killed himself in the world with anything, God will punish him by that same thing on the Day of Judgment.[56]

The Prophet ﷺ also said:

... جندب بن عبد الله في هذا المسجد ... قال قال رسول الله صلى الله عليه وسلم كان فيمن كان قبلكم رجل به جرح فجزع فأخذ سكينا فحز بها يده فما رقأ الدم حتى مات قال الله تعالى بادرني عبدي بنفسه حرمت عليه الجنة

Among those who were before you, there was a man who was inflicted with wounds. He felt despair, so he took a knife and with it he cut his hand; blood kept flowing until the man died. God the Exalted said, "My slave has caused death on himself hurriedly; I forbid Paradise to him."[57]

Narrated Abū Hurayra:

حدثنا حبّان بن موسى: أخبرنا عبد الله: أخبرنا معمر، عن الزهري، عن سعيد بن المسيّب، عن أبي هريرة رضي الله عنه قال: شهدنا مع رسول الله صلى الله عليه وسلم خيبر، فقال رسول الله صلى الله عليه وسلم لرجل ممن معه يدَّعي الإسلام: (هذا من أهل النار) . فلما حضر القتال قاتل الرجل من أشد القتال، وكثرت به الجراح فأثبته، فجاء رجل من أصحاب النبي صلى الله عليه وسلم فقال: يا رسول الله، أرأيت الذي تحدثت أنه من أهل النار، قد قاتل في سبيل الله من أشد القتال، فكثرت به الجراح، فقال النبي صلى الله عليه وسلم: (أما إنه من أهل النار) . فكاد بعض المسلمين يرتاب، فبينما هو على ذلك إذ وجد الرجل ألم الجراح، فأهوى بيده إلى كنانته فانتزع منها سهما فانتحر بها، فاشتد رجال من المسلمين إلى رسول الله صلى الله عليه وسلم فقالوا: يا رسول الله صدّق الله حديثك، قد انتحر فلان

---

[56] Reported by Abū Awānah in his *Mustakhraj* from the hadith of Thābit bin ad-Dahāk. A similar hadith is reported by Abū 'Umrān by al-Bazzār but its chain contains Ishāq ibn Idrīs who is "discarded."

[57] Bukhārī.

فقتل نفسه، فقال رسول الله صلى الله عليه وسلم: (يا بلال، قم فأذّن: لا يدخل الجنة إلا مؤمن، وإن الله ليؤيّد هذا الدين بالرجل الفاجر

We were in the company of God's Messenger ﷺ on an expedition, and he remarked about a man who claimed to be a Muslim, saying, "This (man) is from the people of the (Hell) Fire." When the battle started, the man fought violently until he got wounded. Somebody said, "O God's Apostle! The man whom you described as being from the people of the (Hell) Fire fought violently today and died." The Prophet ﷺ said, "He will go to the (Hell) Fire." Some people were on the point of doubting (the truth of what the Prophet ﷺ had said) while they were in this state, suddenly someone said that he was still alive but severely wounded. When night fell, he lost patience and committed suicide. The Prophet ﷺ was informed of that, and he said, "God is Greater! I testify that I am God's Slave and His Apostle." Then he ordered Bilāl to announce amongst the people: "None will enter Paradise but a Muslim, and God may support this religion (i.e. Islam) even with a disobedient man."

The Prophet ﷺ said:

عن أبي هريرة ... أن رسول الله صلى الله عليه وسلم قال من قتل نفسه بحديدة فحديدته في يده يتوجأ بها في بطنه في نار جهنم خالدا مخلدا فيها أبدا ومن قتل نفسه بسم فسمه في يده يتحساه في نار جهنم خالدا مخلدا فيها أبدا ومن تردى من جبل فقتل نفسه فهو يتردى في نار جهنم خالدا

Whoever throws himself down from a high mountain and kills himself will be throwing himself down from a mountain in the Fire of Hell for all eternity. Whoever takes poison and kills himself will be taking poison in the Fire of Hell for all eternity. Whoever kills himself with a weapon (literally, "iron") will be holding it in his hand and stabbing himself in the stomach in the Fire of Hell for all eternity).[58]

---

[58] Bukhārī.

أخبرنا اسحق بن منصور قال أنبأنا أبو الوليد قال حدثنا أبو خيثمة زهير قال حدثنا سماك عن أبي
سمرة:أن رجلا قتل نفسه بمشاقص فقال رسول الله صلى الله عليه وسلم أما أنا فلا أصلي عليه

A person [engaged in battle] killed himself with a broad-headed arrow.
The Messenger of God

said, "As for me, I will not pray over him."

Even the mufti of the most fundamentalist school of law in Islam, the "Wahhabi/Salafi" school of thought, declared that suicide bombings have never been an accepted method of fighting in Islam. The Mufti of Saudi Arabia, Shaykh 'Abd Al-'Azīz Āl-Shaikh declared, "To my knowledge so-called 'suicide missions' do not have any legal basis in Islam and do not constitute a form of Jihād. I fear that they are nothing but a form of suicide, and suicide is also prohibited in Islam." This echoes an earlier *fatwa* by his predecessor, the late Saudi mufti Shaykh 'Abd Al-'Azīz bin Bāz.

Unfortunately, none of this has stopped the terrorists from employing these tactics. One way they attempt to justify their illicit actions is by citing the story of the Prophet's paternal cousin, az-Zubayr ibn al-'Awwām. During a battle against the Byzantine army, Az-Zubayr said to a group of Muslim soldiers, "Who will promise to go with me and fight our way through the enemy lines until we reach the end of their lines, then go around their camp back to our current position?" A group of fighters said, "we promise." Az-Zubayr led the group into the enemy's lines and fought through their ranks until they reached the Byzantine camp. They then rounded the Byzantine camp and returned to the main body of the Muslim army. The terrorists claim that Az-Zubayr and his men were certain to die, and thus commit suicide while fighting the enemy. In fact, az-Zubayr did not tell his companions "let us kill ourselves." He only exposed himself and his men to what is commonly expected in war—the probability of being killed by the enemy. He did not intend to die, but to fight, and with God's support to win. This is not suicide, rather it is bravery and heroism. Islam has always required perfect chivalry and discipline. For that reason, soldiers are ordered to endure and fight even in the face of tremendous odds. Thus, the so-called "logic" of the terrorists is clearly illogical.

THE PROHIBITION AGAINST INFLICTING "COLLATERAL DAMAGE"

The rest of the terrorists' reasoning is similarly flawed.

Today's militant Islamists cite a ruling by the Shafi'ī scholar al-Mawardī in which he stated that, when involved in combative Jihād, if the enemy has mixed non-combatants among warriors—either by chance or intentionally as "human shields"—then Muslim archers are allowed to fire on the enemy, despite the fact that due to the randomness of shooting, non-combatants might die. The terrorists' use this ruling to justify bomb attacks against civilian areas.

In fact, they are only twisting the law to suit their purposes. This ruling is very specific in that it allows such attacks on the assumption that it is the combatants that are targeted by the archers, not the civilians, who only happen to be present or, worse, are being used as human shields. The assumption of the jurist is also that the Muslims and the enemy are engaged in face-to-face fighting, between combatants. However, the attacks carried out by today's militants do not target combatants; rather, they are typically carried out in public locations more frequented by civilians, including innocent women and children. In Islamic law, one cannot build a case on doubtful assumptions, such as "those people are likely all engaged in fighting Muslims." Such an argument is false, and the result is the killing of innocents without justification.

The Islamic rules of military conduct never permit using civilians as targets or as hostages. In Islam, even so-called "collateral damage" is unacceptable. Therefore, if a Muslim kills himself, along with innocents, it is a doubly forbidden act.

Even the Islamist, Shaykh Yūsuf al-Qaradāwī issued a *fatwa* condemning the tragic suicide attacks of September 11, 2001, stating: "Even in times of war,

Muslims are not allowed to kill anybody save the one who is engaged in face-to-face confrontation with them." He added that they are not allowed to kill women, old persons or children, and that haphazard killing is totally forbidden in Islam. Shaykh Qaradāwī on another occasion defined terrorism as "the killing of innocent people ... with no differentiation between the innocent and the foe."

Another widely followed religious scholar, As-Sayyid Tantāwī, Grand Shaykh of Islam's highest institution of learning, the University of Al-Azhar, has said that attacks against women and children are "not accepted by Islamic law." Al-Azhar's Research Academy, shortly after September 11, 2001, declared that a "Muslim should only fight those who fight him; children, women and the elderly must be spared."

The Prophet 变 said:

> ... *Whoever fights under the banner of a people whose cause is not clear, who gets flared up with family pride, calls people to fight in the cause of their family honor or fights to support his kith and kin, and is killed, then he dies in a state of ignorance (jāhilīyyah).*

> *Whoever indiscriminately attacks my Ummah, killing the righteous and wicked among them, sparing not even those firm in faith, and fulfilling not a pledge made with whoever was given a promise of security, has nothing to do with me and I have nothing to do with him.*[59]

This shows us very clearly, that those who indiscriminately attack both Muslims and non-Muslims by suicide bombings, killing innocent people arbitrarily, are rejected completely by the Prophet 变.

This hadith also makes it abundantly clear that if someone attacks a person whose safety has been guaranteed by the nation's government, the Prophet 变 is abandoning the attacker and dissociating himself from him. For

---

[59] Muslim.

the believer, nothing could be more distressing than for the Prophet ﷺ to abandon him. Yet, today we see beheadings of people who are working to help bring stability, humanitarian aid and human rights to Iraq.

Finally, this hadith demonstrates the Prophet's emphatic opposition to those who would declare a false combative Jihād. Indeed, it represents a very clear prediction by the Prophet ﷺ that a people will arise who will create havoc and confusion, who are arrogant and proud of themselves, and who despite appearances, are in fact fighting for the sake of their families and tribes. Their fight is not Jihād by any means.

Such is the case in many Muslim countries today, including the land of Hijaz, Pakistan, Darfur, Egypt, Algeria, Iraq and so forth. What is taking place in these nations today is clearly described in this hadith: "Whoever indiscriminately attacks my Ummah, killing the righteous and wicked among them, sparing not even those firm in faith."

FALSE RULINGS SUPPORTING SUICIDE ATTACKS

Often those who justify suicide attacks cite as evidence the story of the Companion Al- Barā' ibn Malik at the Battle of Yamāma, in which the Muslims fought Musaylima the Liar, who had begun the war by attacking the Muslims:

The Muslims gained ground against the idolaters the day of Yamāma until they cornered them in a garden in which Musaylima was staying. Al-Barā'ibn Mālik said: "O Muslims, throw me to them!" He was carried aloft until when he was above the wall, he penetrated [the enclosure]. Then he fought them inside the garden until he opened it for the Muslims and the Muslims entered. Then God killed Musaylima.

Al-Barā' threw himself onto them and fought them until he opened the gate after having received more than eighty cuts. Then he was carried away and tended. Khālid [ibn al-Walīd] visited him for a month.[60]

Studying this analogy, one finds that it is not relevant, for in the incident cited the two combatant armies were fighting face-to-face. In the process, Al-Barā' did not kill innocent people. He went over the wall with the intention of either opening the door or dying in the attempt. In fact, his death was expected at the hands of the enemy, not by his own action. This, like the earlier example of az-Zubayr ibn al-'Awwām, is exemplary of chivalry and bravery, not of intent to commit suicide.

PRISONERS OF WAR

In regard to prisoners of war God says:

حَتَّى إِذَا أَثْخَنتُمُوهُمْ فَشُدُّوا الْوَثَاقَ فَإِمَّا مَنًّا بَعْدُ وَإِمَّا فِدَاءً حَتَّى تَضَعَ الْحَرْبُ أَوْزَارَهَا

At length, when ye have thoroughly subdued them, bind a bond firmly (on them): thereafter (is the time for) either generosity or ransom: Until the war lays down its burdens. [47:4]

In a similar vein, the Prophet ﷺ said:

He who gives a promise of safety to a man in regards to his life, then kills him, I am innocent of the actions of the killer, even if the one killed was a disbeliever.

It is established that, though the Prophet ﷺ captured prisoners, he never compelled or forced anyone to embrace Islām. The same holds true for his Companions.

---

[60] The first narration is by Baqi ibn Makhlad in his *Musnad* narrated from Ibn Ishaq. The second is from Thumama, from Anas. Both are cited by Hafiz Ibn Hajar in *al-Isaba fi Tamyiz al-Sahaba*, Vol. 1 p. 279-280.

The Companions of the Messenger of God ﷺ used to ransom captives and rejected killing them saying, "What would we gain from killing them?"

REBELLION AGAINST RULERS

Abū Hanifa's school says that the head of the state, the Imām, cannot be expelled for being a corrupt person (*fāsiq*).[61]

IBN NUJAYM

The scholar Ibn Nujaym said, "It is not permitted for there to be more than one state leader (*Imām*) in a time period. There may be many judges, even in one state, but the leader is one."[62]

AL-BAHJŪRĪ

Al-Bahjūri said, "It is an obligation to obey the leader, even if he is not fair or trustworthy or even if he committed sins or mistakes."[63]

He also said, "… you have to obey the Ruler even if he is oppressive."

This means that neither a group nor an individual is permitted to declare war against the ruler of a nation.

Moreover, in his explanation of *Sahīh Muslim* al-Bahjūrī said, "… it is forbidden to come against the ruler."[64]

---

[61] Imām Abū Hanīfa, *Sharh al-aqā'id an-nasafiyya*, p.180-181.

[62] 62 Ibn al-Nujūm *Al-Ashbah wal-nadhā'ir*, p. 205.

[63] Al-Bahjūrī, *Sharh Sahīh Muslim*, vol. 2, p. 259.

[64] Al-Bahjūrī, *Hashiyyat al-Bahjūrī 'ala sharh al-ghizzi*, vol. 259.

AMIN AHSAN ISLAHI

While commenting on the underlying reasons which form the basis of state authority for combative Jihād, Amin Ahsan Islahi writes:

The first reason [for this condition] is that God Almighty does not like the dissolution and disintegration of even an evil system until a strong probability exists that those who are out to disintegrate the system will provide people with an alternative and a righteous system. Anarchy and disorder are unnatural conditions. In fact, they are so contrary to human nature that even an unjust system is preferable to them …this confidence [that a group will be able to harmonize a disintegrated system and integrate it into a united whole] can be reposed in such a group only as has actually formed a political government and has such control and discipline within the confines of its authority that the group can be termed as *al-Jama'ah* [the State]. Until a group attains this position, it may strive [by religiously allowable means] to become *al-Jama'ah*—and that endeavor would be its Jihād for that time—but it does not have the right to wage an "armed" Jihād.

The second reason is that the import of power which a group engaged in war acquires over the life and property of human beings is so great that the sanction to wield this power cannot be given to a group the control of whose leader over his followers is based merely on his spiritual and religious influence on them [rather than being based on legal authority]. When the control of a leader is based merely on his spiritual and religious influence, there is not sufficient guarantee that the leader will be able to stop his followers from fasād fi'l-arḍ [creating disorder in the society]. Therefore, a religious leader does not have the right to allow his followers to take out their swords [that is to wage an armed struggle] merely on the basis of his spiritual influence over them, for once the sword is unsheathed there is great danger that it will not care for right and wrong and that those who drew it will end up doing all [the wrong which] they had sought to end. Such radical groups as desire revolution and the object of whom is nothing more than disruption of the existing system and deposition of the ruling party to seize power for themselves play such games –

and they can, for in their eyes disruption of a system is no calamity, nor is it cruelty or any kind an evil. Everything is right to them [as long as it serves their purpose].[65]

Hudhayfa bin al-Yaman narrated a hadith in which he said:

يَكُونُ بَعْدِي أَئِمَّةٌ لاَ يَهْتَدُونَ بِهُدَايَ، وَلاَ يَسْتَنُّونَ بِسُنَّتِي، وَسَيَقُومُ فِيهِمْ رِجَالٌ قُلُوبُهُمْ قُلُوبُ الشَّيَاطِينِ فِي جُثْمَانِ إِنْسٍ."

قَالَ: قُلْتُ: كَيْفَ أَصْنَعُ؟ يَا رَسُولَ الله إِنْ أَدْرَكْتُ ذَلِكَ؟ قَالَ: "تَسْمَعُ وَتُطِيعُ لِلأَمِيرِ، وَإِنْ ضُرِبَ ظَهْرُكَ، وَأُخِذَ مَالُكَ، فَاسْمَعْ وَأَطِعْ

The Prophet ﷺ said, "There will be after me leaders who do not follow my guidance and do not follow my Sunnah, and there will be among them men whose hearts are like those of Satan in the body of a human being." And I asked the Prophet ﷺ, "What I should do at that time if I reach it?" He said, "listen and obey the ruler, even if he lashed your back and took your money, listen and obey."[66]

In another narration:

أفلا نقاتلهم؟ قال: لا، ما صلوا " ومن حديث عوف بن مالك رفعه في حديث في هذا المعنى " قلنا يا رسول الله أفلا ننابذهم عند ذلك؟ قال: لا، ما أقاموا الصلاة " وفي رواية له " بالسيف " وزاد " وإذا رأيتم من ولاتكم شيئًا تكرهونه فاكرهوا عمله ولا تنزعوا يدا من طاعة

Auf bin Mālik said, "O Prophet of God, do you recommend that we fight them?" He said, "No, do not fight them as long as they do not prevent you from your prayers. And if you see from them something that you dislike, dislike their acts, do not dislike them. And do not take your hand out from obedience to them."[67]

---

[65] Islahi, Amin Ahsan, *Da'wat-i-Din awr us ka Tariqah-i-kar* (Urdu; ch. 14, pp. 241-2).

[66] *Sahih Muslim.*

[67] *Sahih Muslim.*

It is narrated from 'Abdullāh ibn al-'Abbās that the Prophet ﷺ said:

مَنْ كَرِهَ مِنْ أَمِيرِهِ شَيْئًا فَلْيَصْبِرْ عَلَيْهِ، فَإِنَّهُ لَيْسَ أَحَدٌ مِنَ النَّاسِ خَرَجَ مِنَ السُّلْطَانِ شِبْرًا، فَمَاتَ عَلَيْهِ، إِلَّا مَاتَ مِيتَةً جَاهِلِيَّةً

If someone dislikes his ruler, he must be patient, because if he comes against the ruler in a rebellious or destructive manner by only a handspan and dies, he dies in a state of pre-Islamic ignorance (jāhilīyyah) and sin.[68]

Other hadiths with similar themes are:

سَتَكُونُ عَلَيْكُمْ أَئِمَّةً تَعْرِفُونَ مِنْهُمْ وَتُنْكِرُونَ، فَمَنْ أَنْكَرَ قال أبو داوُدَ قال هِشامٌ بِلِسانِه فَقَدْ بَرِيءَ، وَمَنْ كَرِهَ بِقَلْبِهِ فَقَدْ سَلِمَ وَلَكِنْ مَنْ رَضِيَ وَتَابَعَ يَا رَسُولَ الله أَفَلَا نَقْتُلُهُمْ؟ قال أبو داوُدَ: أَفَلَا نُقَاتِلُهُمْ؟ قال: لَا مَا صَلَّوْا

The Prophet ﷺ said, "There will be upon you leaders who you will recognize and disapprove of; whoever rejects them is free, whoever hates them is safe as opposed to those who are pleased and obey them." They said, "Should we not fight them." He said, "No, as long as they pray."

وعن عوف بن مالك رَضِيَ اللهُ عَنْهُ قال سمعت رَسُولَ اللهِ صَلَّى اللهُ عَلَيْهِ وَسَلَّمَ يقول: ﴿خِيارُ أَئِمَّتِكم الذين تُحبونهم ويحبونكم، وتصلون عليهم ويصلون عليكم. وشِرارُ أَئِمَّتِكم الذين تَبغضونهم ويبغضونكم، وتلعنونهم ويلعنونكم!﴾ قال: قلنا يا رَسُولَ اللهِ أفلا ننابذهم؟ قال: ﴿لا ما أَقاموا فيكم الصلاة، لا، ما أَقاموا فيكم الصلاة. . .﴾

The Prophet ﷺ said, "The best of your leaders are those you love and they love you, you pray for them and they pray for you. The worst of your leaders are those who anger you and you anger them and you curse them and they curse you." We replied, "O Messenger of God, should we not

---

[68] Bukhārī and Muslim.

remove them at that?" He said, *"No, as long as they establish the prayer amongst you...".*[69]

These texts are clear evidence that whoever lives under a government must obey the ruler and live peacefully. Insurrection, or violence by any group against the ruler, is completely rejected in Islam, and was prohibited by the Prophet 鷺 and will be a cause of death on the way of ignorance (*jāhilīyyah*). These hadith refer to the leader of a nation, not the leader of a small group. Therefore, groups that take up violent struggle against their regimes are prohibited in Islam and are, by default, illegal and blameworthy.

The true path to correcting the mistakes of a ruler is according to the hadith:"A most excellent Jihād is when one speaks a word of truth in the presence of a tyrannical ruler."[70] Note here that the hadith does not mention fighting the ruler, but rather praises the one who corrects the ruler by speech.

Unfortunately, we see today countless individuals and groups who label their rulers and their governments apostates or unbelievers, thinking that this gives them an excuse to declare "Jihād" against them. They assert that this is because they do not rule by what was revealed to the Prophet 鷺. Even worse, they terrorize and kill government officers, members of the armed forces and public servants, simply because they are easy targets. These groups use a "militant Islamic" ideology to justify such felonious action, declaring the ruler, the government, and its officers to be criminals standing in the way of "true Islam" who thus must be eliminated.

If the ruler commits wrong, it is not permitted to label him an apostate, nor to indoctrinate people to use militancy to oppose him. In the time of the Prophet 鷺 after the conquest of Makkah, a Companion named Hātib ibn Abī Balta, assisted some of the enemies of Islam by passing them secret information. When questioned as to his motives, Hātib replied:

---

[69] Narrated in Ad-Dārimī's *Sunan* and a similar hadith is related in *Musnad* Ahmad.

[70] Narrated by Abū Saʿīd al-Khudrī in Abū Dawūd and Tirmidhī.

قال: يا رسول الله لا تعجل علي، إني كنت أمراً ملصقا في قريش، ولم أكن من أنفسها، وكان من معك من
المهاجرين لهم قرابات بمكة، يحمون بها أهليهم وأموالهم، فأحببت إذ فاتني ذلك من النسب فيهم، أن
أتخذ عندهم يدا يحمون بها قرابتي، وما فعلت كفرا ولا ارتدادا، ولا رضا بالكفر بعد الإسلام، فقال
رسول الله صلى الله عليه وسلم: (لقد صدقكم)

*O Prophet of God! Do not hasten to give your judgment about
me. I was a man closely connected with the Quraish, but I did
not belong to this tribe, while the other emigrants with you, had
their relatives in Makkah who would protect their dependents
and property. So, I wanted to compensate for my lacking blood
relation to them by doing them a favor so that they might protect
my dependents. I did this neither because of disbelief nor apostasy
nor out of preferring disbelief (kufr) to Islam.*

The Prophet of God 🕮 said, "Hātib has told you the truth."[71]

We see here that the Prophet 🕮, though fully aware of Hātib's actions,
never considered him to be outside the fold of Islam, nor did he inflict any
punishment on him. Regarding Hātib and his support of the unbelievers, God
revealed the following verse:

يَا أَيُّهَا الَّذِينَ آمَنُوا لَا تَتَّخِذُوا عَدُوِّي وَعَدُوَّكُمْ أَوْلِيَاءَ تُلْقُونَ إِلَيْهِم بِالْمَوَدَّةِ وَقَدْ كَفَرُوا بِمَا جَاءَكُم مِّنَ الْحَقِّ
يُخْرِجُونَ الرَّسُولَ وَإِيَّاكُمْ أَن تُؤْمِنُوا بِاللَّهِ رَبِّكُمْ

*"O you who believe! Do not take My enemy and your enemy for
friends: would you offer them love while they deny what has
come to you of the truth, driving out the Messenger and
yourselves because you believe in God, your Lord?"* [60:1]

Though the verse reprimands Hātib, showing him in the wrong, God
nonetheless did not take him out of the state of belief, yet continued to address
him with the honorable title *"you who believe."* This constitutes proof that,
even if someone assists a regime that does not support Islam, one cannot harm

---

[71] Sahīh Bukhārī.

that person, as the Prophet ﷺ did not inflict any punishment on Hātib. One wonders then how so many groups today freely label those working for their governments as renegades and apostates, and issue fierce edicts to kill them. Their work with the government might be for their livelihood, or for building a bridge of trust for the Islamic community to ensure a better future relationship or a better understanding of Islam.

THE INNER JIHĀD

Islam is not a rhetorical religion. It is based on unity, love and rational action. Soon after the Prophet's death, Islam radiated out from its earthly center, the *Ka'aba*, implacable symbol of the faith. Jihād was the dynamic of this expansion. Outwardly, it embodied the power of Islam against error and falsehood; inwardly, it represented the means of spiritual awakening and of transcending the self. Referring to this, the Prophet ﷺ said while returning from battle:

قدمتم خير مقدم، وقدمتم من الجهاد الأصغر إلى الجهاد الأكبر: مجاهدة العبد هواه

We are now returning from the lesser Jihād to the greater Jihād, the Jihād against the self.[72]

The Prophet ﷺ is reported to have said during his Farewell Pilgrimage:

المجاهد من جاهد نفسه في الله

... The fighter in the Way of God is he who makes Jihād against himself (jāhada nafsah) for the sake of obeying God.[73]

God says in the Holy Qur'ān:

---

[72] Ghazali, in the *Ihyā'*; al-'Irāqī said that Bayhaqi related it on the authority of Jābir and said: There is weakness in its chain of transmission. According to Nisā'ī in *al-Kuna* is a saying by Ibrāhīm ibn Ablah.
[73] Tirmidhī, Ahmad, Tabarānī, Ibn Mājah, and al-Hākim.

وَالَّذِينَ جَاهَدُوا فِينَا لَنَهْدِيَنَّهُمْ سُبُلَنَا

Those who have striven for Our sake, We guide them to Our ways. [29:69]

In this verse, God uses a derivative of the linguistic root of the word "Jihād" to describe those who are deserving of guidance, and has made guidance dependent on Jihād against the false desires of the soul. Therefore, the most perfect of people are those who struggle the most against the selfish promptings of the ego for God's sake. The most obligatory Jihād is that waged against the base side of the ego, desires, the devil and the lower world.

The great Sufi Al-Junayd said:

Those who have striven against their desires and repented for God's sake shall be guided to the ways of sincerity. One cannot struggle against his enemy outwardly (i.e. with the sword) except he who struggles against these enemies inwardly. Then whoever is given victory over them will be victorious over his enemy, and whoever is defeated by them, his enemy defeats him.

DHIKR: THE REMEMBRANCE OF GOD

عَنْ أَبِي الدَّرْدَاءِ؛ أَنَّ النَّبِيَّ صلى الله عليه وسلم قَال (أَلَا أُنْبِئُكُمْ بِخَيْرِ أَعْمَالِكُمْ، وَأَرْضَاهَا عِنْدَ
مَلِيكِكُمْ، وَأَرْفِعِهَا فِي دَرَجَاتِكُمْ، وَخَيْرِ لَكُمْ مِنْ إِعْطَاءِ الذَّهَبِ وَالْوَرِقِ، وَمِنْ أَنْ تَلْقَوْا عَدُوَّكُمْ فَتَضْرِبُوا
أَعْنَاقَهُمْ، وَيَضْرِبُوا أَعْنَافَكُمْ؟) قَالُوا: وَمَا ذَاكَ؟ يَا رَسُولَ اللهِ!قَال ذِكْرُ اللهِ

The Prophet ﷺ said: "Shall I tell you something that is the best of all deeds, constitutes the best act of piety in the eyes of your Lord, elevates your rank in the hereafter, and carries more virtue than the spending of gold and silver in the service of God, or taking part in Jihād and slaying or being slain in the path of God?"

They said: "Yes!" He said: "Remembrance of God."[74]

Thus, one finds the principles of the spiritual Jihād are based on eliminating the ugly, selfish and ferocious characteristics of the ego through spiritual training and mastery of *dhikr*, the remembrance of God.

This remembrance takes many forms. Each school of Sufism focuses on a different form of ritual *dhikr* to enable the seeker to approach the Divine Presence, varying from individual, silent recitation and chanting to vocal group sessions. It is this spiritual struggle that raises man and instills in him the sense of relationship with His Creator. It is always calling for love between humanity and striving in God's Way for better understanding between various communities of all faiths. Through this spiritual Jihād, the effect of the selfish ego on the soul of the seeker is removed, uplifting his state from depression, anxiety and loneliness to one of joy, satisfaction and companionship with the Most High.

CONCLUSION AND POLICY RECOMMENDATIONS

It is apparent that the understanding of Jihād as a concept is dismally blurred by the ongoing rhetoric employed by Islamist activists and extremist scholars. Disregarding centuries of classical scholarship and using a simplistic, literal approach to the Qur'ān and the holy traditions of the Prophet 鸒, they have created a convincing picture of Jihād as militant, continuing warfare between the Muslims and non-Muslims—a situation they contend will maintain until the end of time.

The only way to dispel the false notions of Jihād put forth by the extremists, who are extraordinarily well-funded and organized, is an equally strong effort put forth by Muslim governments in re-educating their populations, in particular their youth, about the correct meaning

---

[74] Related on the authority of Abū al-Dardā by Ahmad, Tirmidhī, Ibn Mājah, Ibn Abī al-Dunyā, al-Hākim, Bayhaqī, and Ahmad also related it from Mu'adh ibn Jabal.

and implications of this term. Such efforts must be sustained and ongoing, and must have the support of modern, moderate Muslim scholars in each nation.

I propose the following recommendations for each nation engaging in these re-education efforts:

1) Hold follow-on discussions to create a response to the current abuse of the term Jihād.

2) Stage public presentations to educate the citizenry about this information, based on those discussions.

3) Publish literature, including school textbooks for all ages, explaining the accurate definition of Jihād and distributing this literature in large quantities.

4) Encourage modern, moderate scholars to stand up and speak up in opposition to the extremists.

5) Create national podium for modern, moderate scholars so that their voices may be heard including television spots, radio, and public events.

6) Publish in public media the proceedings of the above-mentioned debates and discussions by modern, moderate scholars.

This effort to educate the Muslim masses about the true meaning of Jihād will, in itself, provide an important contemporary example of its true spirit.

Civilian & Democratic Dimensions of Governance in Islam

by
Professor Mohammad Hashim Kamali, Ph.D.

Dean, International Institute of Islamic Thought & Civilization, Malaysia

Civilian & Democratic Dimensions of Governance in Islam

by Professor Mohammad Hashim Kamali, Ph.D.

Notwithstanding the long history of scholarship on government in Islam, ambiguities and opportunities for debate continue over the basic concepts of state and methods of governance. This essay takes a brief account of these uncertainties and then proceeds to focus on some of the characteristic features of governance in Islam, notably its civilian and democratic dimensions. As part of that discussion, we shall explore the issue of *hudud* [crimes mentioned in the Quran] and the various interpretations of crime and punishment, generally.

I. An Overview of the Various Interpretations of Islamic Governance

Constitutional law is one of the most under-developed areas of *fiqh*, and stands in this respect at the opposite pole of *'ibadat*, on which the *fiqh* is exceedingly elaborate. A great deal of what has been written in the past focuses on the early caliphate and pays little attention to subsequent developments. The literature that has come about as a result is still wanting of critical evaluation and development in conjunction with contemporary conditions. Uncertainties set in at an early stage. The growing *khilafa* of the early decades of Islam had barely realized its potential, when military conflict and the subsequent irregularities of dynastic rule exposed it to intolerable disruptions. The republican features of the *khilafa*, especially consultation (*shura*) and *bay'a*, were only nominally kept and subjugated to the abuses of a totalitarian system, which characterized the many centuries of rule under the Umayyads, the Abbasids and others.

More recently the Islamic revolution of Iran stimulated Islamic scholarship and many researchers have since written on issues of constitutional law in Islam. Yet despite this development, as one observer noted "many issues of interest to Islamic political thought and constitutional law remain shrouded in ambiguity which tend to cause hesitation and impede research." It is perhaps the present generation of researchers who will contribute to the development of constitutional law in a way "that would suit the requirements of our age and address issues of concern to us at present."[1]

A former Mufti of Egypt, Shaykh Ahmad Huraydi, observed that the political order that held sway in the Muslim lands over the greater stretch of history from the Umayyads to the end of the Ottomans did not, on the whole, comply with the principles of Islam, and those who wrote on Islamic government and administration focused their attention on dynastic practices which did not reflect normative principles but only expounded the history of government in those times, and there is "a big difference between the two."[2]

Juristic works on the caliphate are on the whole concerned with the methods of designation of the caliph, his rights and duties and a certain institutional blueprint on the judiciary, vizierate, and departmental structures for the army, taxation, police duties and so forth. This literature on the whole does not address modern developments, including the nation state itself, and constitutional themes on democracy, separation of powers and so forth.

Abu'l-Hassan al-Mawardi's(d.450/1058) renowned *Kitab al-Ahkām al-Sultāniyya*, pays more attention to the realities of the Abbasid state of his time rather than the foundational guidelines of the Qur'ān and Sunna. He pays scant attention to consultation and has no section or chapter on the basic rights of people.

The Qur'ān does not provide a clear text on creating a government body, although it does contain a number of provisions that either take

---

[1] Mohamed Selim el-Awa, *al-Fiqh al-Islami fi Tariq al-Tajdīd*, 2nd edn., Beirut: al-Maktab al-Islami, 1419/1998, p. 44.
[2] Lecture series by Shaykh Ahmad Huraydi held at the University of Cairo – as quoted by Fu'ad A. Ahmad, *Usul Nizam al-Hukm fi'l-Islam*, pp. 15-16.

its existence for granted or help to develop some understanding of its attributes. The basic question as to the formation of a state and whether it is a Qur'ānic requirement as such has, on the whole, received a presumptive and inferential response: Since the Qur'ān requires obedience to "those in charge of the affairs, the *ulu'l-amr*", makes references to *khalifa*, and contains injunctions on war and peace, justice, enjoining good and forbidding evil, commercial transactions, as well as a number of specific rules on punishments and inheritance etc., it is concluded that these cannot be duly implemented without the existence of a government.[3] According to an Islamic legal maxim, the means to a *wajib* also partakes in *wajib*, hence the conclusion that formation of a government is an Islamic obligation. The *ulu'al-amr* may refer to a government, which is more likely, or it could alternatively be said to be alluding to influential community leaders, tribal leaders, religious leaders etc., who may be obeyed and entrusted with making decisions over community affairs.

The juristic position in support of the formation of a system of rule is also said to have been upheld by general consensus, or *ijmā'*, of the companions of the Prophet. The Prophet, peace be on him, himself had not issued clear instructions on the matter of succession to the rule, nor on the subject of government, according to the majority of the Sunnis at least. Only the Shiites have held that the Prophet did nominate Ali Ibn Abu Talib to be the leader after him.

The Constitution of Madina *(dustur al-Madina)* laid down the foundations of a new community under the Prophet's leadership in Madina. Much attention was paid in this document to establishing a basis of cooperation and cohesion between the Emigrants, the Helpers and the Jews. Issues of leadership and subjugation of the powerful tribal structure to the authority of the new government, principles of equality and justice, freedom of religion, right of ownership, freedom of movement and travel and combating crime were among the major

---

[3] Cf. Qamaruddin Khan, *The Political Thoughts of Ibn Taymiyyah*, Islamabad: Islamic Research Institute, reprint 1985, pp. 23-24; Monir Hamid al-Bayati, *al-Nizam al-Siyasi al-Islami Muqarinan bi'd-Dawla al-Qanuniyya*, Baghdad: Dar al-Bashir, n.d, p. 49.

preoccupations of this document. Thus it would appear that the constitution of Madina had civilian characteristics.

Al-Mawardi's writings on caliphate have also been influential. He wrote at a time when the emirs and military rulers had taken over much of the effective power of the caliph of Baghdad. In an attempt to vindicate the caliph, al-Mawardi laid emphasis on his position as the patron of religion. The course of events in Ibn Taymiyya's time (d. 728/1348), notably the fall of Baghdad to the Mongols, marked the practical extinction of the caliphate. Since Ibn Taymiyya found no indication of a caliphate in the Qur'ān or the Sunna, he departed from the premises of the classical theory of *khilafa* . Instead he called attention to the basic principles of Sharī'a and a Sharīa-oriented polity (*siyasa shar'iyya)*, in preference to *khilafa*, which he thought was short-lived and lasted only 30 years. What was important, he emphasized, was commitment to a set of principles that the Sharīa had enunciated. It was this renewed emphasis that characterized Ibn Taymiyya's idea of the Sharīa state, which proved influential. Yet in his perception of *siyasa shar'iyya*, Ibn Taymiyya also marked a move in the direction of a judicious polity that went beyond the Sharīa and envisaged a government that made decisions on the basis of Sharia as well as practical exigencies.

'Abd al-Rahman Ibn Khaldun's (d. 1406) writing on monarchy (*mulk*) and its supporting idea of group solidarity (*asabiyya*) in the ruling circles differed from the juristic approach of the ulama as it was predicated in the recognition and legitimacy, in principle, of hereditary rule that prevailed over the greater part of Islamic history. Ibn Khaldun observed if the Muslim community found it difficult to restore the early *khilafa*, then it should be legitimate for them to establish a secular monarchy (*mulk*) founded on *asabiyya* of the politically dominant group that is guided and restrained by rational laws and the people's welfare. Thus he distinguished between two types of monarchy namely valid monarchy (*mulk haqiqi*) and deficient monarchy (*mulk nāqis*). The former is based on considerations of public interest and rational laws and it provides an acceptable alternative to *khilafa*. *Mulk naqis* is, on the other hand, based in brute force rather than *'asabiyya* and it is destined to decline. Ibn Khaldun thus effectively separated politics from religion and suggested an alternative basis of legitimacy to the *khilafa* which had been abandoned for centuries.[4]

It will be noted that the juristic details and conditions of *khilafa* which occur in the works of al-Mawardi and others do not necessarily embody a religious obligation. Some of these conditions, such as the requirement that the caliph must be from a Quraysh descent, or that he be a *mujtahid*, as well as the proviso that insists on the territorial unity of the caliphate are, in any case, either obsolete or have been amended and changed.

Contemporary writings on the subject of Islamic governance are generally cognizant of the absence of a model and prototype for an Islamic system of rule and tend to lay emphasis on conformity to a set of principles. A government may consequently take a variety of forms and yet qualify Islamic if it complied with those principles.

Salient among these principles are *shura* (consultation) justice, equality, freedom, cooperation (*al-tacawun*) and people's welfare (*maslaha*). Any system of government which implements these ideals, repels turmoil (*fitna*) and establishes peace and order, qualifies as Islamic. It may be similar to the historical models or may be different and combine new features in response to actual developments of modern society.

II. GENERAL CRITERIA & CHARACTERISTICS

Islamic governance may be characterized as civilian (*madaniyya*), which is neither theocratic nor totally secular but has characteristics of its own. It is a limited and a constitutional form of government whose powers are constrained by reference to the injunctions and guidelines of the Qur'ān and the authentic *Sunna*. It is also rooted in the notions of trust (*amana*) and vicegerency (*khilafa*) and its principal assignments are to

---

[4] Muhammad Mahmud Rabi, *The Political Theory of Ibn Khaldun,* Leiden: E.J. Brill, 1967, p. 145f.

administer justice and secure the welfare (*maslaha*) of the people. The state represents the community to which it is accountable. The Islamic system of rule may also be described as a qualified democracy which is elected by the people and must conduct its affairs through consultation. Some of these attributes are elaborated as follows.

II.1 GOVERNMENT AS A TRUST (*AMANT AL-HUKM*)

In a Qur'ānic passage known as the *ayat al-umara'* (the rulers' verse), the text provides:

> "God commands you to render the trusts (*al-amānāt*) to whom they are due, and when you judge among people, you judge with justice." (4:58)

The verse immediately following is also on the same subject as it addresses the Muslims to "obey God and obey the Messenger and those in charge of the affairs among you ..." (4:59).

Muslims are thus enjoined to be faithful in the fulfillment of their trusts, to render impartial justice among people, and obey their lawful rulers. The command over the fulfillment of trusts in this verse is, according to one view, addressed to the leaders of the community and those to whom the community have entrusted with their affairs. Others have held that this verse is addressed to all strata of the people, the ruler and ruled alike.

The broad and unqualified expression '*al-amanat*' in this text characterizes the Islamic system of rule. Government is consequently a trust and its leaders and officials are all the bearers of that trust, and trust is signified, in turn, by the notion of accountability before God and the community. This is also supported by the hadith which provides to the effect:

> "Each of you is a guardian and responsible for that which is in his custody."

The *imam* is a guardian and he is responsible for his subjects, a man is a guardian and he is responsible for his family, a woman is a guardian....

It was on this basis that the Righteous Caliphs understood their positions analogous to guardians and executors over the property of orphans. They saw it as their duty to personally supervise the community affairs, protect their *maslaha* and their rights.

Amana in government is also an integral part of representation. The head of state is a representative (*wakil*) of the community by virtue of *wakalah* which is a fiduciary contract and a *wakil* is simultaneously a trustee. The *wakil* derives his authority from the principal (*muwakkil*) and exercises it on the latter's behalf.

II.2 LIMITED GOVERNMENT, THE RULE OF LAW, & INDIVIDUAL FREEDOMS

Islam advocates a limited government in which the individual enjoys considerable autonomy. Islam does not advocate a totalitarian government as many aspects of civilian life remain outside the domain of law and government. Muslim jurists have thus distinguished the religious (*dini*) from juridical (*qada'i*) obligations and maintained that only the latter are enforceable before the courts. Most of the religious aspects of the individual's life in society are private and non-justiceable. Even some of the religious duties such as prayer, fasting, the *hajj*, and almost all of what is classified as recommendable, reprehensible and permissible (*mandūb, makruh, mubāh*) are not legally enforceable. Government normally plays an administrative and regulatory role in regard to *'ibada*t and should not, without compelling reason, impinge on people's freedom in respect of *mubah, mandub,* and *makruh.* The private and civil rights of the individual are also immune, by the express injunctions of Sharīa, against encroachment by others, including the state. No government agency, nor even the Sharīa courts, has powers to grant discretionary changes in the private rights and properties of individuals, without the consent of the person concerned. Judicial decisions must be based on lawful evidence; free of compulsion and espionage, and the ground of those decisions must also be clearly stated. Trial procedures of Sharia courts and the substance of the Sharia law of evidence are, as such, positivist and civilian in character and do not show significant variation with their parallel procedures in the civil courts.

The state's accountability to the community is in the present day Muslim countries articulated in their written constitutions which have become a common and generally accepted feature of government. These constitutions are essentially instruments of limitation which articulate the state's commitment to uphold and protect the basic rights of people, and are, as such, consistent with Islamic principles.

The powers of state in Islam are also limited in respect of taxation. The Sharīa thus lays down a number of criteria which the government must observe in the imposition of tax: (1) Tax must be just and proportionate to the ability of the taxpayer; (2) it must apply equally to all according to their ability without discrimination; (3) taxation must aim at the minimum of what is deemed necessary; (4) the well-being of the taxpayer must be observed in the determination of quantity and methods of collection; and (5) Taxation must observe the time limit of one calendar year, or similar other periods, for the yield or profit to materialize.[5] Abu Yusuf, al-Mawardi and others have emphasized that tax must be moderate and must in no case deprive the taxpayer of the necessities of life.[6]

Freedom is also an important theme in the ruler and ruled relationship. Freedom has meant different things to different people. To a mystic and Sufi, freedom has primarily signified freedom from the desires of the self and from dependency on the material world. The philosophers and theologians have discussed freedom in the context of predestination and free will and the interplay, so to speak, between the

---

[5] Cf. Abd al-Wahhab Khallaf, *al-Siyasa al-Shariyya*, Cairo: al-Matbaa al-Salafiyya, 1350/1970, p. 59; Umar Chapra, *The Economic System of Islam*, Karachi, University of Karachi Press, 1971, p. 63; Kamali, "Characteristics of the Islamic State," p. 33.

[6] Abu Yusuf Yaqub b. Ibrahim, *Kitab al-Kharaj*, 2nd edn., Cairo: al-Salafiyya, 1352 A.H., p. 152; Abu'l-Hasan al-Mawardi, *Kitab al-Ahkam al-Sultaniyya*, 2nd edn., Cairo: al-Babi al-Halabi, 1386 A.H., p. 194.

human will and the will of God Most High. But the jurist and student of constitutional law have understood freedom in the context of the relationship of ruler to ruled, freedom from authority, and the ability to lead one's life away from the imposition of other individuals and the coercive power of the state.

Islam stands for freedom, which is why it is often characterized as *din al-fitra*, that is, a natural religion, which values a great deal of what is of value to human nature and the enlightened reason of man. Human nature is to a large extent influenced by human intellect, which is probably the most important part of the *fitra* of man. The Qur'an declared in a verse that "God created mankind in the state of nature (or natural freedom). Let there be no change in God's creation."(al-Rum,30:30). The Prophet Muhammad, peace be on him, added his voice to this when he said in a hadith that "every child is born in the natural state (of *fitra*)...." Indeed one of the missions of the Prophet, as the Qur'an put it was "...to remove from the people the burdens and the fetters that were on them before."(al-A'raf,7:157) The caliph 'Umar b. al-Khattab had occasion to pose a question that begged a negative answer: "since when did you enslave the people whom their mothers gave birth to as free individuals?"

II.3 RULE OF LAW IN MATTERS OF CRIME & PUNISHMENT

Islamic criminal law is remarkably flexible in almost all of its parts except for the so-called *hudud* offences, which remains open to legal interpretation and the discretionary punishment of *taazir*. Punishment in Islamic law falls under the general heading of *mu'amalat*, that sphere of the law which is concerned with social affairs and transactions. Unlike devotional matters (*'ibadat*) which are mainly regulated by the text, the *mu'amalat* are open to considerations of public interest and social change. In almost every area of *mu'amalat*, be it commercial law, constitutional law, taxation or international relations, the Sharia lays down some basic rules and leaves the rest to be regulated by human legislation based on *ijmaa*, *shura*, *maslahah* and *ijtihad*. In this way the Sharia itself leaves room for development of laws based on the ordinances of legitimate government and the *uli'l-amr*. As such the Sharia on these matters consists only partially, and in much smaller part for that matter, of divine law.

The judges have no powers to create an offence, without valid evidence in the sources, on discretionary grounds. There is, moreover, no recognition in the Sharia of any privileged individual or group and no one, including the head of state, enjoys any special immunity or status before the courts of justice.

It seems that both the conventional *fiqh* and radical Islamists substantially concur in their perceptions of *hudud*, yet the latter tend to elevate the ranking of *hudud* to one of the first and foremost agenda of an Islamic state. Hudud are the crimes listed in the Qur'an for which there are specific punishments. They include only four offences, namely theft, adultery, slanderous accusation (*qadhf*) and highway robbery (*irabah*). It is important to not that wine-drinking (*shrub*) and apostasy (*riddah*) are not *hudud* crimes and the Qur'an specifies no punishment for these two offences. Yet, *Fiqh* manuals have, erroneously, included *shrub* and *riddah* in the category of *hudud*.

In all the four instances where the Qur'an specifies a punishment, it also makes a provision for repentance and reform. This aspect of the *hudud* has been largely ignored in the juristic discourse of *fiqh*. One can easily argue that the prescribed punishments for these offences are not fixed and mandatory because references to these punishments are immediately followed by provisions on reformation and repentance. Yet, conventional *fiqh* has overlooked this combination and has simply opted for mandatory enforcement.

Let us review the four verses under discussion.

A) THEFT (*SARIQAH*)

"As for the thief, male or female, cut off their hands as retribution for their deed and exemplary punishment from God. And God is exalted in power, Most Wise. But one who repents after his crime and amends his conduct, God redeems him. God is Forgiving, Most Merciful." (5:38-39)

b) Adultery and Fornication (Zina)

"As for the woman and the man guilty of zina, flag each of them one hundred lashes. Let not compassion move you away in their case from carrying out God's law... unless they repent thereafter and amend themselves, then, God is Forgiving, Most Merciful." (24:2-4)

c) Slanderous Accusation (Qadhf)

"And those who accuse chaste women and fail to produce four witnesses, flag them eighty lashes and accept not their testimony ever after, for they are transgressors – except for those who repent thereafter and reform themselves, then, God is Forgiving, Most Merciful." (24:4-6)

d) Highway Robbery (Hirabah)

For this offense the text (5:33) prescribes a three-fold punishment which consists of crucifixion, cutting of limbs and banishment, depending on whether the robber has both killed and robbed his victim or committed the one and not the other crime, or that he only terrorized the people without inflicting any loss of life and property. The text then immediately continues to provide:

> "Except for those who repent before they fell
> into your power, in which case, know that God
> is Forgiving, Most Merciful." (5:33)

The *hudud* issues are lengthy and involved. The present writer has discussed them elsewhere in fuller detail.[7] It is merely submitted here

---

[7] Mohammad Hashim Kamali, *Punishment in Islamic Law: An Enquiry into the Hudud Bill of Kelantan*, Kuala Lumpur: Institute for Policy Studies, 1995; reprint, Kuala Lumpur: Ilmiah Publishers 2000. Malay tr. Ilmiah Publishers 2004. See also *Idem Islamic Law in Malaysia: Issues and Developments*, Kuala Lumpur: Ilmiah Publishers, 2000, 135f.

that repentance and reform is an integral part of the Qur'anic text on these offences, but the jurists simply turned a blind eye to this aspect of the text. They explained their negligence by saying repentance prior to arrest in these offences absolved the offender from punishment in so far as it related to the Right of God (or community's right) content of the offence but not in respect of the Right of Man therein. It is proposed here instead that the text does not draw this line of distinction. If we were to take a holistic approach to the Qur'anic outlook on *hudud*, we would need to make reformation and repentance an integral part of our approach side by side with that of punishment.

The *fiqh* literature on the subject of apostasy has been questioned by many prominent ulama and calls for a corrective by contemporary scholars. The subject of controversy is the sweeping generalization of only ONE circumstantial *hadith* [tradition of the Prophet] to the effect that "one who changes his religion shall be killed." This is obviously inconsistent with the impulse of the Qur'an and its clear proclamation on the freedom of religion. For apostasy occurs in about 20 places in the Qur'an and nowhere has the holy text assigned a temporal punishment for it.

To understand the historical context of that one hadith, note that the Prophet of Islam lived in a continuous state of war with the Quraysh of Makkah. They were engaged in active hostility over a number of years and there were no neutral grounds in those tumultuous relations. A Muslim who became apostate would flee to Makkah, join the enemy forces, and fight against Muslims, or else engaged in active conspiracy against them. It was with this background that the Prophet uttered the *hadith* in question. But the *fiqh* literature has almost turned a blind eye to this crucially important circumstantial factor. The result was that a solitary (*ahad*) *hadith* has been taken so far as to suppress the clear text of the Qur'an on the freedom of religion.

In the matter of religious belief, the Qur'an declared: "let there be no compulsion in religion. Guidance had been made clear from misguidance…." and it was for the individuals to accept it or to reject it (al-Baqara, 2:256). Elsewhere in the text, the Prophet was instructed to tell the disbelievers "…to you is your religion and to me, mine "(al-Kafirun, 99:6). And then in a question that begs a negative answer the Qur'an begins by stating that if God had willed, everyone would have embraced Islam, and then poses this question to the Prophet Muhammad: "…are you then forcing the people to become believers?"(Yunus, 10:99). To paraphrase, God tells His Messenger that "I did not choose to compel any one, are you going to do what I did not?'

If you combine the historical context of the tradition with the injunctions against religious compulsion, it is clear that the corporal punishment for apostasy must be revised.

II.4 Whether a Qualified Democracy

Democracy is basically predicated in a set of principles most important among which are a recognition of the inherent worth of every human being, a representative and participatory government, acceptance of the rule of law, equality of all citizens before the law, and a high level of tolerance of unconventional views and beliefs. Islam contains a set of basic principles which make it highly responsive towards many of the moral and legal prerequisites of democracy. If democracy means a system of governance that is the opposite of dictatorship, Islam is compatible with democracy because there is no place in it for arbitrary rule by one man or a group of men.

The political system in early Islam was neither democratic nor did it rest on absolutism as understood by the Greeks and Romans; it was an Arab system of government to which Islam added its own requirements. Though *shura* was an entrenched Arab practice and essentially democratic, it did not have a binding character. In the history of Islamic government too, *shura* did not constitute a check on the powers of the caliph. The Qur'an on the other hand spoke in high praise of *shura*, to the extent of coming close to making it mandatory. The Madinan state practiced *shura* and it also showed commitment to justice, equality and people's rights, just as it also turned its back, due mainly to the Qur'an, on ethno-centricity of the Arabian culture. These are some of the features of governance in Islam that exhibit harmony with the principles of democracy. The medieval caliphate admittedly set a negative record on many of the democratic features of governance such as *shura, bay'a*, and the egalitarian teachings of Islam. The government was not answerable to the people, nor did it resort to consultation as such, and it turned *bay'a*, to all intents and purposes, into little more than window dressing. Yet hardly anyone has spoken in support of those methods, and the ulama community have generally regarded them as flagrant departures from the valid norm.

It may be stressed also that the Qur'an threw its support behind *shura,* and then the Prophet himself adopted it as a regular feature of his leadership, a pattern that was followed by the Pious Caliphs after him. This would make *shura* a part of the normative precedent. Contemporary conditions also lend support to the normativity of *shura* which has received the blessing of the pioneers of Islam.

The basic harmony between Islam and democracy is manifested in Islam's resolute denunciation of oppressive and arrogant rulers, the Pharaoh and the Kora, who sought to enslave and humiliate their people. The Prophet, peace be on him, expressed this vividly in a hadith: "when you see my community afraid of calling a tyrant "tyrant" then take leave of it." The ruler in Islam is an agent and employee who is accountable to the people. This was amply shown in the speeches and sermons of the first and second caliphs, Abu Bakr and Umar. Bear also in mind that democracy was the fruit of a long-standing struggle in which the people successfully subjugated despotism to the will of the masses.

Political parties are an important feature of modern democracy. As opposed to those who argued that Islam rejects political parties, one may say that the Sharia principles of *hisba* (promotion of good and prevention of evil), and *nasiha* (sincere advice) as well as the people's right to criticize their leaders can all be given a meaningful role within a multi-party system. To curb despotism and oppressive rule is not within the capacity of individuals acting in isolation. But when the people join together in large numbers, they can influence government policy, in which case there should be no need for acts of rebellion and uprising against oppressive rule as often happened in the past. Political parties may thus be said to be acceptable.

Muhammad Iqbal (d. 1938) spoke affirmatively of the democratic impulse of Islam but said that the Muslims never effectively developed the elective principle. This was due partly to the Persians and the Mongols, the two great races which embraced Islam and formed governments; they were not only strangers to the elective principle, but actively opposed to it. The Persians worshipped their monarchs as manifestors of divine power, and the Mongols were given to tribalist methods. Iqbal also wrote: "The republican form of government is not only thoroughly consistent with the spirit of Islam, but has also become a necessity in view of the new forces that are set free in the world of Islam."

Muhammad Asad described the Islamic government democratic and added that democracy as conceived by the West was infinitely nearer to the Islamic conception thereof than to its Greek parallel. For Islam maintains that all human beings are equal and must be given the same opportunities for development and self-expression. Islam essentially envisaged an elective form of government. A government that comes to power by "non-elective means becomes automatically illegal."[8]

CONCLUSION

There is general agreement on the necessity of leadership and a system of rule that manages the community affairs in accordance with the basic principles of Islam, but evidence is inconclusive as to what form and structure it should have. Any government that is committed to the principles of Islam, may consequently be regarded Islamic regardless of the organizational form and model to which it may subscribe. By and large, the rich legacy of *fiqh* we have with us is basically a juristic

---

[8] Muhammad Asad, *The Principles of State and Government in Islam*, Berkeley: University of California Press, 1961, p. 36.

construct that has evolved abreast with the changing conditions of time and place. In their broad outline and objectives, constitutionalism and democracy are in basic harmony with the goals and purposes of Islam.

Theocratic government demands unquestioning obedience of its citizens and that naturally discourages individual freedom. Islam has, on the other hand, recognized the individual's right to freedom to the extent as to enable him to disobey an unlawful command, just as it also restrains the government from issuing such a command and imposing on people's freedom.

Contributors

His Excellency Dato Hishamuddin Tun Hussein

A prominent figure in Malay politics and son of former Prime Minister Hussein Onn, Dato Hishamuddin currently serves as Minister of Education of Malaysia. Prior to his current posting, Dato Hishamuddin was Minister of Youth and Sports under former Prime Minister of Malaysia, Dr. Mahathir.

His Royal Highness Prince Raja Muda Nazrin Shah ibni Sultan Azlan Shah

His Royal Highness Raja Nazrin Shah is the crown prince of Sultan Azlan Shah of Perak, Malaysia. An economist by training, Raja Nazrin also serves as Pro-Chancellor of the University of Malaya and Patron of the Institute of Public Relations Malaysia.

Nazeer Ahmed, Ph.D.

Dr. Nazeer Ahmed is a senior scientist, historian, and a former politician in India. He has held positions on noteworthy U.S. Department of Defense government science projects, including design of the Hubble telescope. Dr. Ahmed has written two internationally-acclaimed books on Islamic civilization entitled *Islam in Global History*. He also serves as the President of WORDE and the Executive Director of American Institute of Islamic History & Culture.

Professor Vincent J. Cornell, Ph.D.

Dr. Vincent Cornell is Director of the Middle East and Islamic Studies Program at the University of Arkansas. Dr. Cornell is a nationally known scholar in Islamic studies whose expertise extends across the entire field, from Islamic history to theology and law. His 1998 book Realm of the Saint: Power and Authority in Moroccan Sufism was praised by a peer reviewer as "the most significant study of the Sufi tradition in Islam to have appeared in the last two decades."

PROFESSOR YUSUF DA COSTA, PH.D.

Dr. Yusuf Da Costa previously served as Head of Faculty of Education for the University of the Western Cape, South Africa. In addition to his continued academic endeavors, Dr. Da Costa is a prominent social activist and learned scholar of Islam. His publications include the book *The Honor of Women in Islam.*

SHAYKH MUHAMMAD HISHAM KABBANI

Shaykh Muhammad Hisham Kabbani is one of the world most renowned scholars of Islamic history and the spiritual science of Sufism. As deputy leader of the Naqshbandi Haqqani Sufi Order, Shaykh Kabbani also serves as guide and teacher to approximately 2 million Muslims throughout the world including Southeast Asia and the United States. His broad network of colleagues, government leaders, and students provides an excellent resource for WORDE to develop its programs.

PROFESSOR MOHAMMAD HASHIM KAMALI, PH.D.

Born in Afghanistan in 1944, Mohammad Hashim Kamali is currently Professor of Islamic law and jurisprudence and Dean of the International Institute of Islamic Thought and Civilization at the International Islamic University Malaysia, Kuala Lumpur. He served as member of the Constitutional Review Commission of Afghanistan, May-September 2003, during which period he was appointed as its Interim Chairman. He is currently on the International Advisory Board of eight academic journals published in Malaysia, USA, Canada, Kuwait, India, and Pakistan. His books, *Principles of Islamic Jurisprudence* (Cambridge, and K.L., 1991 & 1998); Freedom of Expression in Islam (Cambridge, & K.L., 1997 & 1998) and *Islamic Commercial Law: An Analysis of*

Futures and Options (Cambridge, & K.L., 2001) are used as reference books in leading English speaking universities worldwide.

HEDIEH MIRAHMADI, J.D.

Long before the war on terror, the struggle for the soul of Islam had begun in cities across the world, including here in the United States. Hedieh Mirahmadi was inextricably drawn to liberating her co-religionists from the shackles of extremists who systematically suppress such inalienable human rights as the equal treatment of women, free speech, and the freedom of religious expression. As a director of the Islamic Supreme Council of America, she taught Muslim communities around the world how to create vibrant civil society infrastructure, such as setting up community centers, interacting with free media, and even negotiating international business transactions as part of a free market economy. She worked with governments in Central and Southeast Asia to fight corruption, and to empower their people with the intellectual and financial capital that could support a successful democracy.

As Executive Director and founder of the WORDE, Hedieh has combined her political, social and intellectual resources in the Muslim world to create the policy and networks that will transform stifled and oppressed Muslim societies into progressive, self-sustaining, institutions that are the cornerstone of a grass roots democracy.

In 2005, Ms. Mirahmadi will be a visiting Scholar at the American Enterprise Institute.

9 781930 409309